The 20th Century's
Most Influential
HISPANICS

Jennifer Lopez
Entertainer

by Terri Dougherty

LUCENT BOOKS

An imprint of Thomson Gale, a part of The Thomson Corporation

THOMSON
™
GALE

Detroit • New York • San Francisco • New Haven, Conn. • Waterville, Maine • London

For more information, contact:
Lucent Books
27500 Drake Rd.
Farmington Hills, MI 48331-3535
Or you can visit our Internet site at http://www.gale.com

LIBRARY OF CONGRESS CATALOGING-IN-PUBLICATION DATA

Dougherty, Terri.
  Jennifer Lopez: entertainer / by Terri Dougherty.
    p. cm. — (The twentieth century's most influential Hispanics)
  Includes bibliographical references and index.
  ISBN 978-1-4205-0021-9 (hardcover) 1. Lopez, Jennifer, 1970—Juvenile literature.
2. Actors—United States—Biography—Juvenile literature. 3. Singers—United States
—Biography—Juvenile literature. 4. Hispanic American actors—United States—
Biography—Juvenile literature. 5. Hispanic American singers—United States—
Biography—Juvenile literature. I. Title.
  PN2287.L634D68 2008
  791.43'028'092—dc22
  [B]
                                 2007024055

ISBN-10: 1-4205-0021-X

Printed in the United States of America

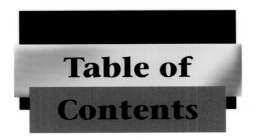

Table of Contents

Foreword

When Alberto Gonzales was a boy living in Texas, he never dreamed he would one day stand next to the president of the United States. Born to poor migrant workers, Gonzales grew up in a two-bedroom house shared by his family of ten. There was no telephone or hot water. Because his parents were too poor to send him to college, Gonzales joined the Air Force, but after two years obtained an appointment to the Air Force Academy and, from there, transferred to Rice University. College was still a time of struggle for Gonzales, who had to sell refreshments in the bleachers during football games to support himself. But he eventually went on to Harvard Law School and rose to prominence in the Texas government. And then one day, decades after rising from his humble beginnings in Texas, he found himself standing next to President George W. Bush at the White House. The president had nominated him to be the nation's first Hispanic attorney general. As he accepted the nomination, Gonzales embraced the president and said, "'Just give me a chance to prove myself'—that is a common prayer for those in my community. Mr. President, thank you for that chance."

Like Gonzales, many Hispanics in America and elsewhere have shed humble beginnings to soar to impressive and previously unreachable heights. In the twenty-first century, influential Hispanic figures can be found worldwide and in all fields of endeavor, including science, politics, education, the arts, sports, religion, and literature. Some accomplishments, like those of musician Carlos Santana or author Alisa Valdes-Rodriguez, have added a much-needed Hispanic voice to the artistic landscape. Others, such as revolutionary Che Guevara or labor leader Dolores Huerta, have spawned international social movements that have enriched the rights of all peoples.

But who exactly is Hispanic? When studying influential Hispanics, it is important to understand what the term actually means. Unlike strictly racial categories like "black" or "Asian," the term "Hispanic" joins a huge swath of people from different countries, religions, and races. The category was first used by the U.S. Census Bureau in 1980 and is used to refer to Spanish-speaking people of any race. Officially, it denotes a person whose ancestry either descends in whole or in part from the people of Spain or from the various peoples of Spanish-speaking Latin America. Often the term "Hispanic" is used synonymously with the term "Latino," but the two actually have slightly different meanings. "Latino" refers only to people from the countries of Latin America, such as Argentina, Brazil, and Venezuela, whether they speak Spanish or Portuguese. Meanwhile, Hispanic refers only to Spanish-speaking peoples but from any Spanish-speaking country, such as Spain, Puerto Rico, or Mexico.

In America, Hispanics are reaching new heights of cultural influence, buying power, and political clout. More than 35 million people identified themselves as Hispanic on the 2000 U.S. census, and there were estimated to be more than 41 million Hispanics in America as of 2006. In the twenty-first century people of Hispanic origin have officially become the nation's largest ethnic minority, outnumbering both blacks and Asians. Hispanics constitute about 13 percent of the nation's total population, and by 2050 their numbers are expected to rise to 102.6 million, at which point they would account for 24 percent of the total population. With growing numbers and expanding influence, Hispanic leaders, artists, politicians, and scientists in America and in other countries are commanding attention like never before.

These unique and fascinating stories are the subjects of The Twentieth Century's Most Influential Hispanics collection from Lucent Books. Each volume in the series critically examines the challenges, accomplishments, and legacy of influential Hispanic figures, many of whom, like Alberto Gonzales, sprang from modest beginnings to achieve groundbreaking goals. The Twentieth Century's Most Influential Hispanics offers vivid narrative, fully documented primary and secondary source quotes, a bibliography, thorough index, and mix of color and black-and-white photographs that enhance each volume and provide excellent starting points for research and discussion.

Introduction

Lovin' la Vida Lopez

G lamorous looks and talent as a dancer, singer, and actress have turned Bronx-born Jennifer Lopez into a superstar. She has conquered movies, music, and the business world, becoming the highest-paid Hispanic actress ever and one of the wealthiest Hispanics in the United States. Her outgoing style adds to her appeal, making her a fascinating public personality.

Lopez is not a typical superstar. She embraces her Puerto Rican heritage and New York upbringing, yet draws fans from many cultures. Her style is all glamour but she remains approachable. Married to Latino superstar Marc Anthony, Lopez is a dreamer and hard worker who achieves what she sets out to accomplish.

Lopez's career is filled with notable accomplishments. She was praised for her portrayal of the slain singer Selena in the movie of the same name, and with audience-pleasing pictures such as *The Wedding Planner* and *Maid in Manhattan* she has become a top box office draw. Commanding a salary of $12 million per film, she has considerable clout in Hollywood.

Music is another arena Lopez has conquered. She has recorded half a dozen CDs, including the multiplatinum *J.Lo* and the all-Spanish *Como Ama una Mujer.* In addition, she is the only entertainer to have

Jennifer Lopez captivates her audience with glamor and talent.

the top-grossing movie and number one nonsoundtrack album in the same week.

With glowing skin, soft, attractive eyes, and carefully coifed hair, Lopez's appearance also contributes to her appeal. Whether she is wearing designer clothing or a comfortable ensemble, she always looks the part of a star. Her fashion sense has made her a regular on the pages of celebrity magazines, and it has made her a successful businesswoman as well. Clothing and perfume lines bearing her name are part of her global business empire.

A Life in the Spotlight

Glamorous looks and success in business, movies, and the recording industry do not account for all of Lopez's appeal. There is a human side to this hard-working actress that makes her all the more intriguing, as Lopez's missteps have earned her just as much recognition as her work. In some ways Lopez is famous for being famous, as her marriages, divorces, relationships, and breakups make headlines as often as her movies and music. She has dated rapper P. Diddy and actor Ben Affleck, and her eye-catching looks made their public appearances together photographic events. A self-confessed romantic, she has been to the altar three times. Her romantic inclinations may not always have worked out for her, but her wrong turns have made this glamorous star more down-to-earth. With her record of relationship miscues it is clear she is imperfect, just like all of the rest of us.

An unguarded personality has made Lopez an interesting figure as well. During her career, which began in the early 1990s, Lopez has learned a great deal about what it means to live a life in the spotlight. Her success took her by surprise early in her career, and she found out quickly that she had to be careful about what she said in interviews. She made some unflattering comments about her costars and other actresses that earned her a poor reputation. Soon stories surfaced about her divalike demands for special treatment, from how her dressing room was decorated to her request for bottled water. She denied that they were true, but the stories persisted. While unflattering, they did keep her in the spotlight. Combined with her public relationships and romantic history, Lopez became known as a star that people wanted to keep an eye on.

Lopez learned to live with the attention she received and refused to compromise her plans for her career. She consistently denied that she was difficult to work with but did not deny that she was driven to succeed. She knew what she expected from herself and admitted she knew exactly what her goals were.

While Lopez has not always been cast in a positive light, she has always been proud of her work, her heritage, and her life. She never stops trying and is a survivor who consistently bounces back after a downturn, whether that downturn is a bad movie or a failed romance.

As her career matured, Lopez learned to minimize its intrusion into her personal life. With her marriage to Anthony she has found the stability she craved. She has also found that she can have a fulfilling career and happy personal life without consistently being in the public spotlight. As a successful actress, singer, and businesswoman, Lopez remains an influential force in the entertainment industry.

Chapter 1

"Jenny from the Block"

Jennifer Lynn Lopez grew up in the Castle Hill neighborhood in the Bronx, New York City, in a close-knit Puerto Rican family. Even as a child she showed a hint of the superstar she was to become. Young Jennifer liked to keep moving. She showed passion and drive at a young age, excelling at whatever she set out to do. From sports to dance, Jennifer devoted energy to her pursuits. Her parents wanted her to channel her drive into law or medicine, but Lopez had her heart set on other things.

Jennifer was born on July 24, 1970. She is the middle child of the family's three daughters. Her sister Leslie is two years older than Jennifer and Lynda is two years younger. Their father, David, was a computer technician for an insurance company, and her mother, Guadalupe, taught kindergarten. Their parents are both from Ponce, Puerto Rico, and came to the United States as young children. They did not meet until they were both living in the Bronx.

The family lived in a tenement home where Jennifer shared a bedroom with her sisters. Both Jennifer's father and mother worked hard. Jennifer's dad worked nights. The family got by but was not wealthy. Their tight financial situation meant that the girls could not afford to buy the latest clothes or shoes.

The Lopezes stressed the value of hard work and encouraged their children to succeed. David's parents had impressed upon him that learning to speak English was an important part of being successful, and he passed that on to his children. Because they wanted their children to learn to speak English fluently, the family spoke English rather than Spanish at home. Their Puerto Rican heritage was also intertwined into their lives, however. They ate David and Guadalupe's favorite Puerto Rican dishes that featured rice and beans, and Jennifer learned some Spanish during visits to her grandmother. Education was important to the family, as was religion. Jennifer's parents wanted to instill solid moral values in their children, and Jennifer and her sisters were not allowed to miss church or school. Guadalupe Lopez did not want her daughters to stray into inappropriate situations, so she kept a close eye on what they were doing.

Although her parents were strict, Jennifer recalls her childhood as a happy one. The family was close and Jennifer's parents loved

Jennifer Lopez's mother, Guadalupe Lopez (center), and Jennifer's sisters, Leslie (left) and Lynda, attend a movie premiere with the superstar singer and actress.

Successful Siblings

Jennifer's sister Leslie became an elementary school music teacher in New York, and Lynda hosted a style show on the E! channel. Lynda began her broadcast career in radio and also was a host of a show on the VH1 channel. She also does entertainment reporting on television.

Since Lynda reports on the entertainment industry, it was only a matter of time before she interviewed her older sister. Jennifer thought it was quite funny to discuss her life with her sister in such a public way. "Here I am talking about boys with my baby sister on television!" she said.

People.com, "Jennifer Lopez: Five Fun Facts." www. people.com/people/jennifer_lopez/0,,,00.html.

their children and wanted what was best for them. "It was a typical Puerto Rican upbringing," Jennifer said. "Lots of music playing and great food."[1]

Music and Dance

Music and dance played a large role in Jennifer's childhood. She began taking dance lessons at the age of five and became involved in Ballet Hispanico, a New York ballet school. She learned ballet, jazz, and flamenco. In addition, she showed an interest in acting and took piano and singing lessons.

Music came into Lopez's life at home as well. There was always music playing in the Lopez house. The family listened to everything from the Top 40 countdown to the Motown sound of the Supremes, Shirelles, and Ronettes. At one time or another salsa, meringue, and doo-wop tunes were all heard in the home. Jennifer admired entertainers such as Barbra Streisand and Diana Ross and hoped to be a star herself one day.

Jennifer's interest in music and dance was also shaped by the musical *West Side Story*. She watched a movie version of the musical over and over again. She loved the film because it featured Hispanic characters. Jennifer and her sisters would act out scenes from the musical, and she always wanted to play the part of the fiery Anita.

When she was young, music and dance were part of Jennifer's daily routine. After classes at the all-girls Holy Family Catholic School were over for the day, Jennifer and her sisters would go to the Kips Bay Boys & Girls Club where Jennifer took dance lessons. Jennifer even helped the younger children at the club. "Even as a kid, Jennifer always wanted to take on more," said Harold Maldonado, director of the Boys and Girls Club. "She wanted to learn more dance routines, try more parts."[2]

Lopez began dancing with Ballet Hispanico (pictured) as a child.

West Side Story *was Lopez's favorite musical. It shaped her interest in music and dance.*

Active Teen

Jennifer did not slow down as she entered her teen years. She and her sisters attended Preston High School, a Catholic high school in the Bronx, where she focused some of her after-school energy on athletics. She participated in gymnastics, softball, tennis, and track. She thrived on competition.

While Jennifer loved sports, she did not neglect her schoolwork. Her parents made sure of this, as they expected her to study hard and get good grades. She did not disappoint them. Even though she preferred athletics, singing, and dancing to studying, she got good grades and finished her homework. Adding dance classes to her schedule made Jennifer a very busy teenager, a foreshadowing of her multifaceted career. Her involvement with dance and sports left little time for just hanging out with a group of friends. "I wasn't a big hanger-outer," she said. "I had my one girlfriend who always came over, or I went to her house. We always had something going on. I was very into tennis and track and field, and I'd go to practice every day and to the meets on the weekend."[3]

Accepting Challenges

Jennifer's interest in sports fit well with her competitive nature. Her father recalled that Jennifer and her sisters were all talented, but Jennifer had something more. Something in her personality always made her push a little harder. Jennifer's involvement in high school track was one example of her determination. She had never tried track before but did not hesitate to join the team. She eventually became so good at the sport that she competed at Madison Square Garden. Her coach mentioned that she had Olympic-level potential.

Doing something that was difficult or challenging did not bother Jennifer. She simply persevered until she succeeded. When she was a high school student she attempted a sewing project that involved turning a pair of jeans into a skirt. It was a difficult process, but she worked on the project until she got it right. "To people, it looked like, 'Oh, she's good at making clothes.' But it was hard! I figured it out because I didn't give up,"[4] she said.

Making Choices

Although Jennifer had many talents, she also realized that she could not do everything and do it well. She needed to keep her grades up, and sports and dance both demanded a commitment of her time. In order to do her best Jennifer had to decide which one she wanted to seriously pursue.

Even though her track coach urged her to continue with the sport, her gut feeling told her she was better suited for dance. "I wanted to achieve something important, and I had to realize that I couldn't be great at track and dance at the same time," she says. "I had to go with what was organic to me, what felt natural. And to me, at that time, dancing and singing and acting felt better."[5]

Rebellion

Jennifer loved her family and did well in school and sports. Her parents preferred that she stay home when she was not busy with classes or her after-school activities, and when she was younger she did not mind obeying them. However, when she turned sixteen she began to get restless.

When Jennifer developed an interest in boys, her parents' restrictions began to seem confining. She disagreed with their rules that kept her from spending more time with kids her own age. She did not want to disappoint her parents, but at the same time she wanted the freedom to head out of the house more often and make more of her own decisions.

Mother and Father Knew Best

"Our parents had a strong work ethic—there wasn't really any other way. They led by example. They would tell us we could never miss a day of work—and they didn't. They told us we had to go to church every week, which they did. They never had any down-time. I didn't realize people were any different until I was a teenager."

—Lynda Lopez, quoted in Anthony Bozza, "Jennifer the Conqueror," *Rolling Stone*, February 15, 2001, p. 44.

Jennifer began to see romance as another challenge. Although her parents did not approve, she began going out with a boy named David Cruz. It became her goal to sneak out and be with her boyfriend. "I was always climbing out windows, jumping off roofs, and he was sneaking up," she told a reporter with a laugh. "It was crazy."[6]

Career Plans

Jennifer also disagreed with her parents when it came to her career plans. After high school, they wanted their smart and ambitious daughter to put her energy into college. They wanted her to go to law school or perhaps become a doctor. Jennifer did not agree with their dreams for her future. She was intelligent and motivated, but her interests did not lean toward law or medicine. At one time she thought about becoming a beautician, but the performing arts had captured her heart. A career in dance was where she wanted to focus her energy.

After high school, Lopez's love of dancing led her to concentrate on a career in the performing arts.

Lopez's first appearance on television was as a dancer on the show In Living Color, *whose cast is shown here.*

homesick and spent the majority of her paycheck on airline tickets as she flew home almost every weekend. Homesickness was not enough to make her give up on her dream, however. Although she was miserable at times, she did not let that keep her from showing up for work.

The Star of the Sister Act

"She really was always one of those people who was great at everything—almost one of those people you hate. In sports, she was this amazing gymnast and shortstop, a great tennis player. Basically, anything she wants to do, she'll be as successful as you can at it. That's the kind of person she is."

—Lynda Lopez, quoted in Anthony Bozza, "Jennifer the Conqueror," *Rolling Stone*, February 15, 2001, p. 44.

Things got better for Lopez during her second year on the show. She rekindled her relationship with her high school boyfriend, David Cruz, and he moved out to California and found work as a production assistant. Having him there made life on the West Coast more bearable for Lopez and improved her career. Now she felt comfortable and stable at home and was no longer distracted by feelings of homesickness. She concentrated more fully on her job and devoted all her energy to it.

On Her Way

While working on *In Living Color*, Lopez continued to take acting classes and began finding work on other television shows. She auditioned for many roles and did not get them, and money was painfully tight. At times a failed audition for a small role meant she was late with her rent. Although work was not always easy to come by, she did not give up on her dream.

As Lopez began to get more television acting roles, she left *In Living Color*. She was on several less-than-stellar television shows such as the series *South Central* and the movie *Nurses on the Line: The Crash of Flight 7*. She occasionally returned to New York to take part in a theatrical show when a television show went on hiatus, usually around holiday time. Although the television shows she appeared in did not do particularly well, Lopez was attracting some notice. When the series *Second Chances* was cancelled, the producers thought enough of Lopez's talent to continue her character in another show.

In pursuit of her goal as an actress, Lopez showed the same determination as a performer she had as a high school athlete. She was not one to let her parents' disapproval or her own homesickness derail her career. She knew where she wanted her career to go, believed she had the talent to take it there, and was driven to achieve and succeed.

While Lopez did not gain celebrity status from her television roles, she did not lack for work. When acting jobs were not coming her way she turned to dancing, backing Janet Jackson on her tour and in the video "That's the Way Love Goes." "You knew that she wasn't going to be part of the chorus very long," said choreographer Tina Landon, who cast Lopez as a dancer in the video in 1993. "She exuded the attitude that one day she was going to be in front."[7]

Chapter 2

Leading Lady

Lopez continued her steady climb toward her goal of becoming a successful actress. She made her first movies, getting her big break by winning the part of singer Selena over hundreds of other actresses. After slipping perfectly into the role of the Latina star whose life ended in tragedy, Lopez was seen as a star on the rise. She had also nabbed roles opposite big-name costars such as Jack Nicholson, Robin Williams, and Sean Penn and established her box office appeal. Lopez's personality and glamorous style also attracted attention, and she became known as a fresh, brash, and talented actress.

Mi Familia

Lopez's big-screen debut came in 1995 in the movie *My Family*/Mi Familia. Jimmy Smits starred in this film that followed three generations of a family that immigrated to the United States from Mexico. The film took the family from the 1920s to the 1970s. Lopez played the family's matriarch, Maria, in the first part of the movie.

The movie was applauded for its subject matter, as it looked at the experiences of a Mexican American family and examined the cultural conflicts the family encountered. Reviewer Roger Ebert enjoyed the film for the warm family sentiments it portrayed. "Gregory Nava's *My Family* is like a family dinner with everybody crowded around the table, remembering good times and bad, honoring those who went before, worrying about those still to come,"[8] he said.

Lopez had a small but interesting role. Her character is married with two children and pregnant with a third when she is sent to Mexico with thousands of other Mexican Americans. She bravely makes her way back to the United States with her baby.

Lopez's portrayal was stirring enough to attract attention. She was nominated for best supporting actress in the Independent Spirit Awards for her role as Maria. These awards honor independent films. The role also allowed her to make some important contacts in the movie industry. One of the executive producers on the film was Francis Ford Coppola. He was a powerful figure in Hollywood, the director of movie classics such as *The Godfather* film trilogy and *Apocalypse Now*. Having him on board as a producer for her first movie was not a bad connection for the young actress to make. In addition, the film was directed by Gregory Nava, who had been nominated for an Academy Award

The movie Mi Familia *marked Lopez's big-screen debut.*

as a writer. He was impressed enough by Lopez's acting to consider her for future roles in his movies.

Money Train

Lopez's other big-screen performance that year was in a very different type of film. Rather than a heart-tugging family story that spanned generations, *Money Train* was an action film set in a New York subway during the Christmas holiday season. It was violent and loud, relying a great deal on crashes and stunt work to move the story along.

Getting an "A" for Attitude

"She's striking, strong, and has an extremely enthusiastic attitude. She's there at 7 in the morning, ready to rehearse, knows all her lines, is fearless about doing her own stunts, whether it's climbing a mountain or tussling in a fight scene."

—Oliver Stone, quoted in Jeffrey Ressner, "Born to Play the Tejano Queen," *Time Canada*, p. 53.

Amid the movie's mayhem Lopez managed to stand out, although she was not the star. She had the female lead in the film, but actors Wesley Snipes and Woody Harrelson got top billing. They had been paired in the popular basketball movie *White Men Can't Jump* and returned to the screen together to see if the friendly contrast between their personalities could once again make a movie work.

In *Money Train* Snipes and Harrelson played foster brothers who work as New York City Transit Authority policemen. A disagreement with their boss and trouble with a loan shark lead to the pair plotting to steal money from a New York subway train. Lopez played another transit authority officer who becomes romantically involved with both brothers, and she got to play love scenes as well as box with Snipes. She managed to rise above a mediocre role, reviewer Ken Tucker said. "Lopez's role is stupidly written . . . but she still gives a smashing performance anyway," he wrote. He was less kind in his assessment of the film, calling it "a big, noisy headache of a movie."[9]

Wesley Snipes and Woody Harrelson appeared with Lopez in the movie Money Train.

The movie had a big budget and paid its two stars millions, so despite poor reviews it got a good deal of publicity. A feisty side of Lopez's personality emerged in the press as this movie was publicized. She was called "fresh and brash" for refusing to carry a revolver but instead preferring to carry a 9mm handgun like her male costars.

The movie also received negative publicity. The subway token booth attacks shown in the film were mimicked in real life, and a subway booth attendant suffered life-threatening burns. Senator Bob Dole encouraged people to boycott the film. Lopez was surprised her movies could have that type of effect on people. "It just made me more conscious of what I would do in other movies," she said. "You have such an influence over people, it's kinda scary."[10]

Big-Name Costars

Lopez's manager, Benny Medina, was helping her make the transition from backup dancer to movie star. She did not get every role she tried out for but made the most of the ones she did. She was savvy about which parts to take in order to help her career. She did not want to take roles that would typecast her as a Latina.

With a good agent and a solid reputation from her previous movie work, Lopez continued to be called in for auditions. She was considered for a variety of roles and her performances received praise, even if the movies she was featured in did not. The movie *Jack*, directed by Coppola, cast Robin Williams as a ten-year-old boy who aged four times as fast as normal. Lopez played his understanding teacher. Film critic Roger Ebert noted that Williams's scene with Lopez was the most tender part of the movie. "The way the teacher tactfully and gently handles the situation is an illustration of a path the whole movie could have taken, had it been more ambitious,"[11] he said in a review that gave the movie 1½ out of 4 stars.

Ebert was more approving of Lopez's next picture, *Blood and Wine*, which starred Jack Nicholson. She played his romantic interest in the 1997 film in which Nicholson played a married wine dealer who steals a diamond necklace. Nicholson's attention to detail in his performance made the movie a good one, Ebert said, and noted that relationships between the supporting characters, of which Lopez was one, made it even better.

A Star Who Keeps Shining

"It's impossible for people to imagine how overwhelming stardom can be. Everybody that this happens to has a period where they have to learn how to deal with it. Jennifer's very level-headed, and she's going to come through all of that with bells on."

—Gregory Nava, quoted in Degen Pener, "From Here to Divinity," *Entertainment Weekly,* October 9, 1998, p. 28.

Lopez received praise for her ability to do what it took to get a movie made when she was filming *U Turn*, which starred Sean Penn and was directed by Oliver Stone. Lopez was not Stone's first choice for the female lead in the movie; actress Sharon Stone had been offered the part but rejected it. Lopez was happy to take the role, however, and impressed Stone with her toughness while filming the movie's gritty scenes. Stone noted that for days she did scenes in which she was barefoot and coated with fake blood.

Despite Lopez's determination, Stone's reputation as a director, and a cast that included experienced stars, the movie received mixed reviews. The suspenseful film cast Nick Nolte as Lopez's husband, who hires Penn to kill her. The movie included some bitter humor and wry commentary on human nature but was criticized for its raw brutality.

Difficult but Successful

Lopez was taking challenging roles. When opportunities arose to work with established directors and stars and take on demanding parts, she took them. Her work as a supporting actress laid the foundation for her first lead role.

Nava, whom Lopez had worked with in *Mi Familia,* was looking for an actress to play the title role in the movie *Selena.* It chronicled the tragic life and career of Selena Quintanilla, a young Tejano singer murdered by the president of her fan club. While Nava was familiar with Lopez's work, getting the role was not easy for her. Lopez had to compete against hundreds of other actresses for the part.

The most difficult part of the auditions was the final callbacks in Los Angeles. Selena's father attended them, and because he had input on the casting selection Lopez knew she had to make a good impression. She felt uncomfortable having him in the room for such a personal portrayal of his daughter, but used that feeling to put emotion into her reading. She got the part.

The movie established Lopez as a star in her own right. In getting the lead role, Lopez became the first Latin actress since Rita Hayworth to take a lead part in a major Hollywood film. She also became the highest-paid Latina actress ever, making $1 million for her role. Some were concerned that she did not look enough like the singer to pull off the role and also about whether someone of Puerto Rican descent should play a person with Mexican roots, but Lopez took on the character's personality and made the portrayal work. Her director supported her. When people criticized her ethnic heritage, he directed attention toward her talent and increasing popularity. "[The criticism] was a little hurtful," director Nava said. "[The protesters] should be celebrating that we have an all-Latino cast and that Jennifer Lopez, one of our own, is becoming a star."[12]

Selena, a movie about singer Selena Quintanilla, showcased Lopez's talents as an actress.

Selena

Lopez's preparation for the role was intense, as she tried to get the character's nuances down perfectly. She lived with Selena's family to study for the role and learned how the singer interacted with those closest to her. "I didn't want to merely impersonate or caricature her," Lopez said. "I wanted to capture her personality, down to the tiniest details—even the way she rubbed her nose."[13]

Nava was familiar with Lopez's dedication and ability from her work on *My Family*/Mi Familia. He complimented her for her ability to concentrate on her role. Despite knowing that her character would ultimately be murdered, Lopez wanted to emphasize the vibrancy of Selena's life rather than the sadness of her sudden death. She did not break down until she saw the finished film.

Any concerns about Lopez's ability to portray the young singer were erased by her dedication to the role. Her hard work came across on-screen, as the movie was praised. "Jennifer Lopez excels as Selena,"[14] wrote Peter Travers in *Rolling Stone*. She received even more recognition for the role when she was nominated for a Golden Globe Award for best performance by an actress in a motion picture.

Marriage Not the Answer

While Lopez basked in the glow of success that *Selena* brought, she began dating Ojani Noa, a model who worked at the restaurant Larios on the Beach, owned by singer Gloria Estefan. They met while she was making *Blood and Wine* in Florida. After a few months of dating he proposed to her in front of the entire movie crew of *Selena* in 1996.

They married in 1997, but the stability Lopez had longed for did not last long, as her increasing popularity almost immediately put a strain on their relationship. It was difficult for Lopez's husband to accept her dedication to her work, and eventually Lopez's skyrocketing career caused her marriage to crumble. What was good for her career was bad for their marriage, and Lopez admitted that her glamorous image and work as an actress made married life difficult. She knew she had to keep working in order to afford the lifestyle she wanted to have, and her commitment to her work put stress on their relationship. Her husband had to deal with her doing love scenes with her costars and wearing revealing clothing. She saw it as part of the business she was in, but her husband did not see it that way.

Lopez and Noa divorced after a year of marriage, although she continued to support him in the restaurant business. They had been in love, Lopez said, but realized that a marriage needed more than that. Compromise, sacrifice, and understanding were also

Jennifer Lopez attends a fashion show with husband Ojani Noa. The couple later divorced.

No Smoking or Drinking

Lopez was always careful to take care of herself. She avoided alcohol and was strongly antidrug. She did not understand people who abused their bodies and always wanted to be on top of her game. Getting drunk or high and spending a lot of time at parties was just not a good use of her time, she reasoned. "I saw it as a distraction for people—a distraction from success," she said. "I had other plans."

When she was young she was too focused on what she wanted to do with her life to waste time drinking, and she felt the same way as her career progressed. "Sometimes I'll have some champagne when somebody makes a toast," she says. "But I'll never finish it. I just never really got into drinking. And now I don't have the time. I don't have the three minutes it takes to smoke a cigarette!"

Elizabeth Kuster, "The Secrets of Jennifer Lopez," *Cosmo Girl*, June/July 2002, p. 86.

Anthony Bozza, "Jennifer the Conqueror," *Rolling Stone*, February 15, 2001, p. 151.

critical, and the couple could not seem to find enough to make their relationship work.

Despite the repercussions it had on her personal life, Lopez was not going to tone down her career plans. She was extremely ambitious and wanted to be more than an actress and dancer. She wanted it all, she told a reporter for *Entertainment Weekly*. "I want everything. I want family. I want to do good work. I want love. I want to be comfortable," she says. "I think of people like Cher and Bette Midler and Diana Ross and Barbra Streisand. That's always been the kind of career I'd hoped to have. I want it all."[15]

Out of Sight

Lopez's success with *Selena* helped establish her as a solid leading lady. She again had a prominent role in her next movie, although it was in a very different type of motion picture. In the action-oriented thriller *Out of Sight* Lopez starred with George Clooney and Ving Rhames as a federal marshal named Karen Sisco, who is assigned to capture two escaped convicts. Her character ends up falling for Jack Foley, played by Clooney.

There was some pressure on Lopez and the others involved with the movie to deliver a successful product. The crime drama, directed by Steven Soderbergh, had to live up to its big stars and big budget. It cost $48 million to make, and Lopez earned $2 million for her role.

The resulting film proved to be worth the investment. Reviewer Peter Travers questioned the wisdom of casting Lopez and Clooney as the movie's romantic leads, but admitted that the pairing worked. "*Out of Sight* shouldn't work, but it does, like a charm," Travers wrote, adding, "From the moment Jack and Karen meet— he's just broken out of prison; she's just failed to stop him with a shotgun—there's a connection."[16] Both Clooney and Lopez were praised for their acting. Lopez "contributes a personal best by

George Clooney and Jennifer Lopez appear in a scene from the action-thriller Out of Sight.

making the tough, sexy Fed—a heroine who could have seemed utterly implausible— both credible and irresistible,"[17] wrote David Ansen of *Newsweek*.

Sudden Stardom

Turning in notable performances in a touching biography and a big-budget action movie took Lopez from supporting actress to star. Recognition followed, and Lopez quickly became a sought-after subject for magazine covers and television interviews. Her face was no longer anonymous.

Suddenly there was a new level of interest in who she was, what she did, and the movies she made. She was no longer an unknown actress. Privacy was a thing of the past, as people knew her name when she walked down the street.

It seemed to Lopez that this rush of recognition poured down quickly. Not too long ago she had been an actress who had ached for the chance to perform and worked hard to build a career. While she had hoped for success, at the same time she had not expected the intense interest in her personal life that came with increased popularity. Her loss of privacy was a surprise. She reacted to this sudden stardom by having anxiety attacks—her heart would begin to beat and her breath would get short. As she became more accustomed to her star status, the anxiety attacks subsided.

In Control

While Lopez was not used to dealing with the public side of her stardom, the recognition she was receiving was an asset to her career. Even when she made a movie that did not generate good reviews, it did not derail her career. Lopez had a role in the mediocre horror film *Anaconda,* which did not do anything to earn her praise for her acting but showed that she was versatile, if nothing else. In a lukewarm review of the movie, Lisa Schwarzbaum called Lopez "the season's hardest working woman in showbiz."[18]

Lopez said she felt fortunate to have had such different roles to play. Latina actresses were often stereotyped as streetwise tough girls, but Lopez had been able to break into a variety of parts.

"Still, there aren't a lot of parts for us, and we're not generally considered for other roles that aren't race specific," she said. "It's starting to change a little bit, but we're still treated like foreigners who just got here because we're not white. We're as American as they come!"[19]

Anaconda got mediocre reviews but showed Lopez's versatility as an actress. She appears here in a scene with Ice Cube.

Glamorous Image

It was not only Lopez's acting ability that drew attention. Her style and looks also made her the center of attention. She was named one of *People* magazine's "50 Most Beautiful People in the World" in 1997. "She has a tremendous amount of glamour, which I haven't seen in an actress in years,"[20] said Edward James Olmos, her costar in *Selena*.

There was no doubt Lopez was a star on the rise. In 1999, when she was again named as one of *People* magazine's "50 Most Beautiful People in the World," *Out of Sight* director Soderbergh commented on her charisma. "Jennifer is one of those people who, when they enter a room, change the molecular activity," Soderbergh said. "It's some kind of spirit, some kind of life force that moves with her."[21]

Confident and Criticized

Lopez was not one to deny that her career was hot and she was a superstar. She was extremely self-confident and had a high opinion of her ability. Being humble about her talent did not seem necessary when her fame and success so clearly indicated that she deserved the recognition she was getting. "People don't believe it yet, but right now I'm very underpaid,"[22] she said.

Lopez did not hold back when asked to give her opinion of other actors and actresses. She called Cameron Diaz a "lucky model," and said Gwyneth Paltrow was popular only because she was dating Brad Pitt. She said she had to rebuff the romantic advances of both Harrelson and Snipes when they made the movie *Money Train* and that Snipes had not taken the rejection kindly. "His ego was totally bruised," she said. "Actors are used to getting their own way." She was not shy about assessing Madonna's ability as an actress, either. "Do I think she's a great performer? Yeah. A great actress? No," she said. "Acting is what I do so I'm harder on people when they say, 'Oh, I can do that—I can act.'"[23]

Lopez's frankness, as well as her opinion of her own ability, made others see her as being self-absorbed. Her self-confidence was seen as egotism, and newspapers ran headlines such as "The Ego Has Landed"[24] and "Glow? It's Just Her Ego Reflecting Off Her Head."[25]

Dressing with Confidence

Lopez had a head-turning sense of style and caused a stir even when she did not mean to. When she and Sean "P. Diddy" Combs appeared together at the Grammy Awards in 2000, she wore a low-cut dress that made people stop and stare. She liked the flowing dress but did not expect the stir it generated. She had simply seen the dress on others before, liked it, and felt it flattered her figure. She did not expect it to make as much of an impact as it did, she said.

No matter what she was wearing, Lopez always looked poised. When she appeared on the Jay Leno show a few years later, she walked in wearing incredibly high-heeled shoes, her skin glowing, and her hair dramatically curled. Her style reflected her self-confidence. It wordlessly told people that she knew how to carry herself. "You've got to know the business you're in," she says. "I don't let anybody tell me what I can and can't do. I just go out there and see what I can and can't do."

Quoted in Juliann Garey, "J. Lo's Great New Year," *Redbook,* January 2002, p. 58.

Adjusting to Fame

As she became more accustomed to being in the spotlight, Lopez tried to manage her reputation more effectively. She learned not to be too candid during interviews. She kept her opinions to herself. She had learned the hard way the difference a few harsh words could make. While she knew she needed to be self-confident when auditioning for a role, she also came to realize that everything she had could rapidly evaporate. She did not think she deserved to have everything come her way, and thanked God for her success.

Although she was called a diva, Lopez did not feel that title fit her. She was self-assured and focused on her career but said she did not treat others poorly. "I have a problem with the term," she said. "I feel like it means that you are mean to people, that you look down on people, and I'm not that type of person."[26]

One thing Lopez would not do was try to change who she was. If she did not feel that her actions were out of place, she was not one to conform to the standards that other people expected of a star. She was going to be herself.

Lopez knew this was part of her appeal. She had something to offer that was uniquely her. Her look, accent, and mannerisms contributed to her style, and they were not things she was about to change. She still had the common sense of the girl who had grown up in the Bronx without nice clothes or shoes. She had grown into an actress who was sensible enough not to be swept away by her stardom, yet savvy enough to take advantage of the opportunities it brought her.

Lopez did not always make the right decisions, and this made her interesting. The lesson in public relations she had received did not slow her career. After doing voice work for the animated movie *Antz,* Lopez took a risk and used her clout to add another facet to her career: singing.

Chapter 3

J. Lo

The movies *Selena* and *Out of Sight* had made Lopez a bankable movie star, but she wanted to do more with her career. She wanted to be a singer as well, and making an album became her next goal. Lopez's dancing ability made her a natural performer, and although singing was something she had never tried professionally, she did not hesitate to give it a try.

It did not take her long to convince music industry executives that this was a good idea. Tommy Mottola, the chairman and CEO of Sony, believed Lopez could be a star singer as well as a top actress. He had his producers talk to Lopez and convince her that they would do all they could to promote her singing career. It only took one meeting with Lopez for a Sony executive to decide that he wanted to sign Lopez to a contract.

Lopez spent a year in the studio recording the CD, and her work ethic impressed Mottola. "I knew she could dance, and I knew she could act," he said. "Once I heard her sing, I thought, Man, here she is, the ultimate superstar. But this is the thing: She doesn't let any of it go to her head. She shows up on time, ready to roll up her sleeves."[27]

Lopez was as picky about her music as she was about her stylish image. Top people in the music industry, such as Sean "P. Diddy" Combs and Rodney Jerkins worked on the album. Singer Marc Anthony was brought in for a Spanish-language duet. Lopez also contributed to the album's song list. Lopez, who had improved her Spanish-speaking skills as an adult, wanted her music to reflect who she was. With her music venture, Lopez tried to deliver music she described as "Latin soul," a combination of Latin music, R & B, and pop. She recorded her demo album in Spanish and included several Spanish-language tracks on her new CD. She titled it *On the 6*, after the subway train Lopez took from the Bronx to Manhattan when she was younger. "You have to follow your heart," she said. "If I had made an album of music that wasn't a reflection of me and it had done well, that would kill me more than if I had done this album and it didn't do well."[28]

Combs helped Lopez on the album and was a supporter of her singing career. He was part of her personal life as well, as they dated from 1999 to 2001. In private, he did not see her as a singer but as someone he cared about. "Jennifer Lopez is my soul-mate. When we're together, I don't see her as a singer or anything like that," he said. "Behind closed doors, she's Jennifer and I'm Sean."[29]

While Lopez and Combs were confident that venturing into music was a good way for her to enhance her career, not everyone agreed. Some, including her own manager, wondered if she was sacrificing a successful movie career in order to try something new. Lopez, however, never wavered. "When I wanted to make my first album [*On the 6*]," she says, "a lot of people were like, 'Don't do it. Your movie career is just starting to take off— why are you going to stop for a year and a half?' And I said, 'Because I want to. I want people to see me for all the things I could be, not for just what they think I could be.'"[30]

Successful Debut

On the 6 was released in 1999 and first spawned the hit single "If You Had My Love," which spent five weeks at the top of the music charts. Once the album was released, more than 2 million copies were sold before the end of its first year. The Spanish-language "No Me Ames" with Marc Anthony rose to the top of Billboard's Hot Latin Tracks chart.

While listeners liked what they heard, however, critics were not as impressed. Lopez was criticized for having a thin, ordinary voice and an album of soft ballads and tame pop tunes. "For all the wads of money spent on her fledgling musical career, Lopez comes across as little more than a Mild Spice Girl,"[31] wrote reviewer David Browne.

Although the album did not receive stellar reviews, that did not prevent it from selling well. Part of its success was due to Lopez's tireless promotion of the album. She spent almost a month

At times, fans had a higher opinion of Lopez's singing than critics did.

in Europe doing interviews with television stations and newspapers. In the United States she visited radio stations, went on television talk shows and awards shows, and did magazine interviews. She was nurturing her acting career at this time as well but made time to squeeze in the appearances before she had to start working on her next movie. "It's been crazy juggling both aspects of my career," she said. "But having a hit record is a dream come true, so I'm happy to work as hard as necessary to keep it going."[32]

J.Lo

Lopez followed *On the 6* with an even more impressive CD, *J.Lo*. The album took only three months to record. "She changed drastically, in a good way, from the last record," producer Cory Rooney said. "Last album, she had to be convinced, even eighty percent through, that she could do it. On this one, she brought technique and control. She knew how important it was to take time on certain songs and rest herself. She had her thing together—you'd've thought she'd been doing it all her life."[33]

In a World of Her Own

"She knows exactly what she wants—and she wants to have it, down to the most minute detail. She says, 'The world is my oyster, and I'm gonna eat it.'"

—Matthew McConaughey, quoted in Juliann Garey, "J. Lo's Great New Year," *Redbook*, January 2002, p. 58.

Lopez wrote four songs for *J.Lo* and continued to exercise control over her singing career. She continued to reach into her past for inspiration, making herself out to be a girl from the Bronx rather than a star. She put a street edge on the dance-pop songs "Love Don't Cost a Thing" and "I'm Real." She again paid attention to the album's details: When she saw a mock-up of the artwork for the album, she suggested ways to move things around and make the lettering more interesting.

Her careful scrutiny paid off, as the singles "Love Don't Cost a Thing" and "I'm Real" were hits, and the album reached multiplatinum sales levels. Critics liked *J.Lo* more than her first effort.

Reviewer Chuck Arnold said, "She doesn't reach for higher meaning or emotional depth on such feel-good party jams as *Play* and *Walking on Sunshine*,"[34] and noted that the songs on the album sounded like Lopez was just having fun.

Lopez found time to tour to support her singing career. A concert in Puerto Rico was taped for a 2001 television special, and *Jennifer Lopez in Concert* aired in 2001. Her determination and strong personality came across onstage as she ended her performances with a steamy glare. "It gets the point across that she's not to be messed with,"[35] said reviewer Erik Pedersen of the *Hollywood Reporter.*

Role Model

Lopez had the confidence to be a strong performer and great entertainer yet continued to struggle with fame and the way it interfered in her most personal issues, including her own body. Lopez's curvy body had been a topic of conversation since the early days of her career, and even her manager questioned whether she should lose weight. Her fuller body type was not considered ideal in a town that valued thinness, and while this at first made her feel self-conscious, she ultimately came to the conclusion that she had to please no one except herself.

Lopez was proud to offer something different. She loved her curvy body, exercised, and watched what she ate. She did not ban foods from her diet, although she ate in moderation. She disagreed when her manager suggested she lose weight. She did not want to try to look like an ultrathin model because that was not her. She was Jennifer, a woman with a healthy body image. "I had grown up around women who were not what you saw in magazines," she said. "They were curvaceous, and to me they were beautiful, you know what I mean? I felt good about myself."[36]

Box Office Attraction

Jennifer's insistence on remaining herself seemed to agree with her fans. While she was drawing fans to the dance floor with her songs, she was also pulling them into the theater to see her movies. In 2000 she made *The Cell* with Vince Vaughn and was paid $2 million for

For her role in the box office hit movie The Cell, *Lopez earned $2 million.*

her role in the psychological thriller. She proved that she earned her paycheck when the movie became a success at the box office. With its strong showing Lopez proved that she could "open" a picture; she was a star whose name brought people to the theater. In a review of *The Cell* Peter Travers says, "It was astute of [director Tarsem Singh] to cast Lopez, an underrated actress with the kind of warmth and magnetism than an audience will follow everywhere."[37]

The next year Lopez again got good reviews for her portrayal of a tough cop in the movie *Angel Eyes*. The film itself was nothing special, reviewer Leah Rozen said, but noted that Lopez's performance outshone the film's average qualities. "In playing hard-edged officers of the law, here and in the far superior *Out of Sight*, Lopez has found an on-screen occupation that provides an effective showcase for her tough-girl urban persona," Rozen said. Her bottom-line review of the film was "High on J. Lo but low on *Eyes*."[38]

Lopez was not one to have a one-dimensional career. She moved into a different movie realm with her next picture, *The Wedding Planner*. In this 2001 romantic comedy, Lopez successfully eased into a light, breezy role opposite Matthew McConaughy. She made $9 million for her role as an ambitious, efficient, and extremely organized woman who is thrown for a loop by love.

The plot was easy to follow: Lopez played a wedding planner who meets a handsome man who turns out to be the groom of the wedding she is organizing. Despite the fact that he is about to be married, they cannot help falling in love. While critics said the movie's plot was too contrived and awkward, audiences disagreed, and *The Wedding Planner* rose to the top of the box office. Despite a poor review of the movie as a whole, critic Roger Ebert enjoyed Lopez's performance, saying, "Lopez pulls her share of the load, looking genuinely smitten by this guy and convincingly crushed when his secret is revealed."[39]

On Top

The success of *The Wedding Planner* propelled Lopez to a new level of stardom. She had proved once again that her name brought people to see a movie, and she had experienced success outside her acting career as well. In 2001 she became the first actress to have a movie and an album on the top of the charts in the same

The popularity of The Wedding Planner *demonstrated that Lopez was a huge draw at the box office.*

week, as *The Wedding Planner* and the CD *J.Lo* both rose to the number one position.

It seemed that everything Lopez attached her name to enjoyed commercial success. "I feel like I haven't even started yet. I'm looking forward to the ninth album, the thirtieth movie," she said. "I want to write more songs, tour, find the right roles, have my own family. That's why I have so much energy. I know what lies ahead."[40]

Business Ventures

Lopez was aware that her name could be used to sell more than CDs and make a movie a success. She knew her image and popularity could expand her horizons. In addition to her career in the entertainment industry, she entered the business world. True to her multitasking style, she began several ventures within a short period of time: a clothing line, a perfume, and a restaurant.

Wonder Woman

"She's got 12 jobs, right? This woman works. What an incredible force Jennifer Lopez has become."

—Actress Vivica Fox, quoted in *USA Today,* "J. Lo's Meal Ticket," April 15, 2002.

Her glamorous looks had always been part of her image, so it seemed only natural that Lopez launch her own clothing line. Andy Hilfiger designed the clothes for the JLO clothing line, which ranged from $20 T-shirts to an $850 leather miniskirt. She used the same hands-on approach with her clothing line as she did with her singing and acting career, paying attention to everything from the styles to the models' makeup and poses for a photo shoot. Her curvy figure had always been part of her image, and she had her clothing line designed with women with real bodies in mind.

She had input to her signature scent as well, a perfume called Glow. She carefully selected a scent that reflected her glamorous image as well as her less affluent past. When she was growing up she had liked an Avon scent called Pearls and Lace, and her mother had worn a spicier perfume called Charlie. She wanted to cap-

Jennifer Lopez, center, models an outfit from her new clothing line.

ture those soft, clean smells in her own scent, striving for something that smelled like fresh air or the ocean.

Lopez also opened a restaurant, Madre's, in Pasadena, California, which reflected her heritage. The restaurant's name meant "mother's" in Spanish and it featured Latin food, the dishes Lopez loved while she was growing up. She brought in her ex-husband, Noa, to manage the place and gave it a comfortable, homey atmosphere. She took care to make sure every detail was to her liking, right down to the shape of the salt shakers.

The restaurant reflected the glamorous side of Lopez's life as well. When it opened, a number of stars appeared at the restaurant. Nicole Kidman, Jay Leno, Kobe Bryant, Brooke Shields, and Ben Affleck were all there to celebrate the event.

Gracious Hostess

While Lopez's busy life left her little time for entertaining, she was a homebody at heart. Although her appearances on the red carpet and in trendy nightclubs were widely publicized, what she treasured was a quiet evening at home.

In an article in *InStyle* magazine, Lopez offered her advice as a hostess. She suggested that the decorations should have a color scheme, and flowers and a beautiful arrangement on the table should be part of the decor, so people will want to sit down and talk and laugh. "I like cooking some of the meal after my guests have arrived, that way people get to hang out in the kitchen," she said. "For background music I usually go for something mid-tempo and soulful like Maxwell or Sade."

Quoted in *InStyle*, "J. Lo's Rules for Life," January 2003, p. 161.

Too Busy?

Lopez's multitasking caused some to wonder about her commitment. Doing so many things could prevent her from doing any of them well. Director Michael Apted had reservations when she was cast in the movie *Enough* because she canceled and rescheduled several meetings with him. However, his attitude changed once filming began and he saw how focused she could be. "Once we started, she was never distracted," he said. "I have never in my career worked with an actor or actress who had such complete focus. Whatever business she was doing, she never brought it on the set. She came prepared and ready to go."[41]

She put effort into everything she did, but with all that she had going on Lopez did begin to falter. Despite handling other projects Lopez put a great deal of energy into her role as an abused wife in *Enough*, and the demanding part was almost too much for her. She was so drained from the energy she had to put into the role and her other work that she went to a doctor with concerns over her stress level and exhaustion. He said she simply needed to get some rest. Lopez took his suggestion and stayed in bed for

Lopez celebrates the grand opening of her new Latin restaurant, Madre's.

P. Diddy

Lopez had a high-profile two-year relationship with rapper Sean "P. Diddy" Combs. Combs was the head of the Bad Boy Records label and also owned restaurants, a music publishing company, and a music studio. He was a rapper whose records went platinum several times over and a producer for hip-hop artists such as Mary J. Blige.

Between 1999 and 2001 Lopez and Diddy collaborated on her recordings and dated as well. They met when Lopez made an appearance in one of his music videos and found they had much in common. Both were from New York and had working-class backgrounds, and both had big dreams for their careers. They also shared a relentless drive to succeed and were driven to put a great deal of energy into achieving their goals.

They became known for their fancy clothes and visits to trendy clubs. Lopez was not a drinker and was more of a homebody than the outgoing Combs, but that did not keep them from heading out together to the hottest nightspots. Their differences became a plus, Lopez said, as they balanced each other.

J. Highs and J. Lows

"You have this irresistibly beautiful woman with so much going on in her life but with so many crash-and-burn moments when it comes to love. It gives some people a sense of comfort: 'Here's somebody who has it all and can't get it together, so I don't feel so bad about myself.'"

—Dennie Hughes, quoted in Cesar G. Soriano, "The Media Have Insatiable Appetite for J. Lo," *USA Today*, June 17, 2004, p. 1d.

It was impossible for them to keep their relationship private, as their appearances in public were widely photographed and reported on. They were seen as the good girl and the bad boy, which made for interesting story fodder. She did not seem to be from his world, yet she wore the glitzy hip-hop diamond watch and cross necklace he gave her. When she walked the red carpet with him in a revealing low-cut dress at the Grammy Awards, everyone took notice.

The relationship between Jennifer Lopez and rapper Sean "P. Diddy" Combs got a lot of attention in the media.

One incident was especially troublesome. Late in 1999 Lopez and Combs were partying at a nightclub with some friends. As Combs and Lopez were leaving, an argument broke out between members of Combs's entourage and another group of people. Shots were fired by a member of Combs's entourage, and three people were hit by bullets. Combs and Lopez left in an SUV, but police later stopped the vehicle, found a gun in it, and took them to the police station.

Lopez was kept there for fourteen hours before being released. Combs, rapper Jamal "Shyne" Barrow, and Combs's bodyguard Anthony Jones were charged in connection with the shooting incident and were later released on bail. Combs was charged with gun possession and later with bribery, after his chauffeur said Combs offered to give him a fifty-thousand-dollar ring if he said

Lopez leaves the district attorney's office after appearing before a grand jury investigating charges against Combs and others.

the gun was his. Jones was also charged with weapons possession and bribery, while Barrow was charged with assault and weapons charges.

The case went to trial in early 2001, and it was at first thought that Lopez would have to testify as a witness. However, Combs said he did not want to put her through that, and she did not appear in court. The trial took two months, and after deliberating for twenty-three hours the jury found Combs and Jones not guilty. Barrow was convicted of assault and weapons charges and was later sentenced to ten years for his role in the shooting.

The strain of the trial was too much for Lopez and Combs's relationship. In the midst of the trial, on Valentine's Day, Combs announced that their relationship was over. Earlier, Lopez had said that it was easier for her to have a relationship with someone who was in the public eye, because he understood what she went through in her career and her dealings with the press. However, after the shooting their relationship began to crack under the strain of the publicity surrounding the trial. Lopez longed for some privacy but realized that the lack of it was likely something she would have to learn to live with. "In this business, your soul is so public and open and out there for everybody. There is no privacy. There really isn't," she said. "At the end of the day, you really have to fight to keep certain things sacred so that they survive. And sometimes they don't, and that's life, but you try."[44]

It was a difficult time for Lopez as she dealt with the emotionally draining trial and her busy career. "We were in a very public relationship—that didn't help," Combs said. "Then, during the trial, we had to be apart a lot, which made it easy to stray. I couldn't be at her door with flowers and cards. A relationship needs that or someone else will step in."[45]

Brief Marriage

As her relationship with Combs ended, Lopez quickly found another. She began dating Judd, whom she had met on the set of her video for "Love Don't Cost a Thing." The quiet performer was much different from the flamboyant Combs. In a life that was chaotic and stressful, he provided the stability she was looking for.

Lopez mingled their romance with her work. They were together in Puerto Rico as he choreographed her concerts there. He visited her on the set of her next movie, *Enough*, and they were openly affectionate.

There were some concerns about how quickly their relationship progressed. Some questioned Lopez's wisdom in moving into another relationship so soon after her breakup with Combs, but she was following her heart. After eight months of dating, the two married in a small ceremony in September 2001 at a secret location in the mountains of California. The romantic wedding included ten thousand rosebuds, one hundred candles, and a seven-tier chocolate and vanilla wedding cake. Their life together began in a high-style fashion. They honeymooned in Italy, where fashion designer Donatella Versace made them guests of honor at a fashion show and dinner and loaned them the use of her villa for a week.

Moving On

Their marriage had a glamorous beginning, but the shine soon faded. The comfort and stability Judd provided to Lopez were not enough to hold their relationship together. Lopez was occupied with her restaurant, her clothing line, an album, and her next movie project, and her busy schedule made for tension in their relationship. Judd kept a low profile and did not move in the same celebrity circles as his wife. Lopez's career overshadowed her husband's, and there was little time for them to be together.

Their worlds ultimately proved to be too different, and their marriage began to falter after only a few months. The couple separated in summer 2002. Their divorce became final in January 2003.

Lopez admitted that matters of the heart tended to be her stumbling block. It seemed that she had control over everything in her life except her love life. She planned the many facets of her career and was extremely careful about her groomed and glamorous image, but in love she often took a wrong turn. "You know," she said, shortly after marrying Judd, "people who know me have always said that the only place I'm vulnerable is in my love life. I've always operated from my heart. That's what inspires me to

Photographers capture a happy moment during the wedding of Jennifer Lopez and Cris Judd.

sing and dance or act or get up in the morning. That's who I am. Therein lies my vulnerability."[46]

Bennifer Begins

As her relationship with Judd cooled, Lopez again became involved with another man almost immediately. She met Ben Affleck on the set of the movie *Gigli*, and the pair began to appear together in public. Soon they were the darlings of the tabloid press, which followed their every move and dubbed them "Bennifer." Lopez's relationship with Affleck consumed her personal life for two years, and it seemed that every nuance of their time together was captured by the press.

They were open about their feelings for each other. When she won a ShoWest Award for female star of the year, he took out an ad in the *Hollywood Reporter* that praised her spirit, talent, poise, and grace. Lopez later appeared on the *Oprah Winfrey Show* and told Oprah that they had not expected to hit it off when they first met. "We both really kind of surprised each other," she said. "I just thought, you know, he was one of these Hollywood guys, [but] he was just, like, a really down-to-earth, charming, sweet, affectionate person."[47]

Ben and Jen Team Up

"I only wish I were lucky enough to be in all your movies."

—Ben Affleck, quoted in Ting Yu et al., "Ben to Jen: Goodwill Gushing," *People*, April 15, 2002, p. 20.

They also attracted attention with their spending habits. Their lavish gifts included a diamond bracelet from Affleck to Lopez and a Ferrari from Lopez to Affleck. In September 2002 he proposed, giving her a pink diamond ring that cost $1.2 million, and speculation began about when and where they would wed.

Lopez had no regrets about the decisions she had made in her personal life. "It might look to the outside world that I've made mistakes, but I don't regret anything," she said. "I've always followed my heart and it's never steered me wrong. One thing I've

The press began referring to Jennifer Lopez and Ben Affleck as "Bennifer."

Jet-Set Schedule

Lopez's life was so busy that she compared herself to Dorothy in *The Wizard of Oz*. Her life, she said, was like being in a tornado. She constantly woke up and found herself in a new place. In 2003, in *Esquire* magazine, she described one particular twelve-day period:

Friday: Works on *An Unfinished Life* with Robert Redford in British Columbia. Flies to Los Angeles with Ben Affleck, her boyfriend at the time.

Saturday: Works in Los Angeles.

Sunday: Attends Lakers game in Los Angeles. Flies back to Vancouver with Affleck.

Monday: Meetings in Vancouver, rehearsals for *Shall We Dance?* Flies to New York in the evening.

Tuesday: Meets with HBO executives about a documentary she wants to produce. Visits NBC, discusses deal with Telemundo. Flies back to Vancouver at night.

Wednesday: Rehearsals for *Shall We Dance?*

Thursday: Magazine shoot, from 9 A.M. to 7 P.M.

Friday: More *Shall We Dance?* rehearsals. Flies to Savannah, Georgia, at night.

Saturday: Goes to see the movie *The Matrix.* Gets a throbbing toothache.

Sunday: Root canal.

Monday: Flies back to British Columbia.

Tuesday: Back at work.

learned as I've gotten older is that you just don't have control over everything. And that's okay. I'm not the type of person to just sit there. . . . I have to move on. No matter how hard things get."[48]

Self-Confident or Egotistical?

Lopez found herself defending her self-assured attitude as well as her relationships. Stories continued to circulate about her diva-like behavior, such as asking for white muslin and white lilies to go with the white walls in her dressing room. Her water, it was said, needed to be room temperature. At a magazine photo shoot, she asked for champagne.

Lopez consistently found herself defending her attitude and actions. She admitted she knew what she liked but did not think of her demands as excessive. The stories were exaggerated, she said. "Almost 100 percent of the diva stuff the press comes up with is false. I don't understand why they say I have 30 bodyguards or ask for certain sheets in rooms," she said. "Anyone who's worked with me knows that I don't have this kind of behavior."[49]

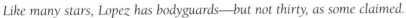

Like many stars, Lopez has bodyguards—but not thirty, as some claimed.

She received public support from her costars and directors. Rather than deriding her requests, they praised her work ethic. Vince Vaughn, who worked with her on the movie *The Cell*, said he saw no evidence of the spoiled diva she was rumored to be. "Never did I see Jennifer take advantage of her position, or belittle or bully anyone," he said. "I think she's handling everything with a lot of grace."[50] Ralph Fiennes acted opposite Lopez in *Maid in Manhattan* and said she did not act like a diva. "She's completely cool, professional,"[51] he said.

Fueling the Interest

In some ways Lopez was responsible for the amount of interest her personal life and attitude generated. She did not always hide the life she was leading. In New York's Central Park, Lopez and Affleck grabbed a kiss between filming scenes for *Jersey Girl*, a film starring Affleck. When a celebrity ball needed an auction item from Lopez, she gave the organization a plate she painted herself that said that she loved Affleck.

Lopez was not above using her relationship with Affleck to further her career. In 2002 she released the CD *This Is Me . . . Then*, which included a reference to her relationship with Affleck in the song "Dear Ben." He also appeared with her in the video for "Jenny from the Block." They were joined by a crowd of celebrities at a party celebrating the release of her movie *Maid in Manhattan*, and they appeared together in summer 2003 to promote their movie *Gigli*. She also had a small role in Affleck's film *Jersey Girl*.

Knocked Down, Getting Up

The couple's popularity meant that their wedding preparations were carefully scrutinized as they planned a $2-million affair. When they visited Savannah, Georgia, and the Hamptons region of New England, rumors spread that they were looking for homes or a spot to marry. After the date of their marriage was leaked to the press as September 14, 2003, the newspaper *USA Today* ran daily updates on their wedding details. A British tabloid offered $1.5 million for photos of the nuptials.

When it seemed that everything from the designer of Lopez's dress to the design of the wedding invitations had been reported

Seeing Is Believing?

Lopez persistently dealt with exaggerated stories about her in the tabloids. She understood, however, how people could be swayed by the headlines they saw. She admitted that she read the headlines on publications such as the *National Enquirer* when she was in the supermarket. "It'll say 'So-and-So's Battle with Such-and-Such.'

And I think, Really? It's probably a lie— I know how many lies they print about me." Even though she knew it was untrue, however, she could not help being taken in by the headline and surprised by the stories' revelations.

Quoted in James Patrick Herman, "J. Lo on a High," *InStyle*, January 2003, p. 154.

upon, a surprising announcement was made. On September 10 the pair postponed the wedding ceremony. The intense public interest that had followed their relationship from the beginning was one of the reasons they decided not to go through with the wedding as they had planned. The postponement, they said, was due to intense scrutiny from the press. "We didn't anticipate the degree to which it would sort of metastasize and become this gigantic story,"[52] Affleck said. The public's interest in their relationship contributed to its ending. Lopez and Affleck had an on-and-off relationship for another few months and then officially broke up in January 2004. After their wedding ceremony had been called off, the press remained interested in the state of the pair's relationship, but Lopez shied away from the spotlight. Public interest in her personal life may have helped her remain a sought-after celebrity, but it also highlighted the painful moments in her life.

No matter how wounded her heart and image might be, she managed to return. "We believe in fairy tales," she said. "We want to find Prince Charming."[53] Lopez was a survivor and was respected because of it.

Chapter 5

Cool Critics,
Warm Public

As Lopez maneuvered through ups and downs in her personal life, her red-hot career began to cool. Once a star who received consistent praise from critics and a warm welcome from audiences at the box office, she began to encounter biting criticism for her acting and indifference from moviegoers. Her singing career hit a lull as well, as her third CD received mixed reviews.

Enough

The first in Lopez's string of disappointing films was *Enough*, released in 2002. She starred opposite Billy Campbell in the drama, playing a woman trying to escape her violent husband. After failing to find freedom through the legal system, she learns the martial art of Krav Maga in order to defend herself.

The role was a dramatic one, but Lopez did not seem to have her heart in the difficult role of an abused wife, said critic Claudia Puig. "*Enough* is too much," wrote Puig in *USA Today*, giving the movie 1½ out of 4 stars. "The hackneyed story about an affluent damsel in distress who decides to fight her bully of a husband is simply too overdone."[54]

In the film Enough, *Lopez plays an abused wife who takes up a martial art so she can protect herself.*

Critic Philip Kerr compared her disappointing performance to her tumultuous personal life. "Clearly, if Lopez does have any talent at all, then it is a talent for making bad choices with her men and her movies," he said. He added that her performance lacked the expression that could have turned it into a gem. "Watching this woman try and put some emotion on her face is a little like watching a toddler trying to put on make-up," he said. "It's a shame, because a film like this ought to have provided Lopez with a real opportunity to prove herself as an actress."[55]

More Criticism

Lopez fared little better in reviews for her next movie, *Maid in Manhattan*. She was paired with Fiennes in a movie about a senator who falls in love with a maid. With the romantic angle and a Cinderella-like theme that had Lopez transform from plain to stunning, the movie had a premise that seemed certain to be a winner.

Critics were lukewarm about *Maid in Manhattan*, however. Rozen called it "a labored romantic comedy about a hotel maid who strikes sparks with a dreamboat politician." She said the script was familiar and reminiscent of other rags-to-riches films such as *Pretty Woman* and *Working Girl*. While she did not like the movie as a whole, she did say that "Lopez, though stiff, brings sincerity and warmth to her role."[56] David Noh of *Film Journal International* faulted director Wayne Wang for using movie clichés such as sentimental songs. The movie was bland, he said, and although it showcased Lopez, it never really took off romantically.

While critics were not happy with *Maid*, audiences disagreed. The lure of Lopez in a romantic comedy was a strong one, and *Maid in Manhattan* topped the box office in its debut week, bringing in $18.7 million. It ultimately brought in the highest lifetime gross of any of her movies.

While audiences liked her in *Maid* they agreed wholeheartedly with the poor reviews for her next film, *Gigli*. She starred with Affleck in the movie about a thug who resorts to kidnapping a mentally challenged boy to keep his mobster boss out of jail. Affleck played the thug, Lopez played another criminal who has to help him keep the kidnapped boy from being discovered, and audiences stayed away. After two weeks of dismal performances in theaters, the headline in the movie industry newspaper *Variety* read, "Auds Give *Gigli* the Cold Shoulder."[57]

It was a movie so bad that critics did not hold back at all in saying how rotten it was. "This misguided romantic comedy goes wrong so often and in such profoundly lunkheaded ways that to say it stinks would be bordering on polite understatement, akin to labeling an irked skunk as fairly fragrant,"[58] Rozen said. The movie was boring, the plot distasteful, and Lopez's acting too smug, she said. Travers agreed that Lopez and Affleck's attitudes detracted from an already bad movie. "The stars display zip chemistry but radiate self-love," he said. "They're so taken with each other that they don't need an audience. Good thing, because they're not going to get one, not with this stinker."[59]

In addition to being roundly panned, the film received numerous Razzie awards. The awards are given to the worst movies of

Gigli was awarded several Razzies, including one for worst picture of 2003.

the year, and *Gigli* won for worst film, worst actor, worst actress, worst screen couple, worst screenplay, and worst director. The movie did set one record: It was the first movie ever to sweep these awards.

High-Profile Pairings

Despite a streak of poor movie reviews, Lopez continued to be a sought-after actress. She was an energetic worker and a high-profile performer who still had the potential to make the right movie a success. She continued her career as an actress by working with some established costars.

Bouncing Back

"As its title may suggest, *This is Me . . . Then* is very much in keeping with Lopez's previous work in both music and film, in that it emphasizes that strength and femininity aren't mutually exclusive assets. The bonus here is the revelation that even two short-lived marriages and a flurry of tabloid headlines can't dull a gal's appetite for romance."

—Quoted in Elysa Gardner, "J. Lo's 'This is Me' Focuses Pop Soul on This Ben Dude," *USA Today*, November 26, 2002, p. 01d.

In 2004 she was paired with Richard Gere in *Shall We Dance?* Gere had successfully played the lead in romantic films such as *Pretty Woman* and *An Officer and a Gentleman*, but here it was a love for dance that was the basis for the film. Gere's character found that dancing added joy to his otherwise ordinary life, and Lopez played his dance instructor. Rozen enjoyed Gere's graceful performance but said that Lopez did not put enough expression into her role. "The actress seemingly keys her performance to her hairstyle," Rozen said. "If her tresses are pulled back tight, she is tense; letting her locks down, she loosens up."[60]

Lopez's string of poor reviews was noted by Roger Ebert when he took a look at her next film, *An Unfinished Life*. He asked that moviegoers see her performance with an open mind. "Give Lopez your permission to be good again; she is the same actress now as when we thought her so new and fine,"[61] he said.

Lopez was cast opposite Robert Redford in the movie, playing his son's widow who reluctantly moves in with her former father-in-law to escape an abusive boyfriend. The movie was made in 2003 and released in 2005, and although delays rarely improve a movie, Ebert gave it three stars. Reviewer Lisa Schwarzbaum, in *Entertainment Weekly,* however, was not as impressed and gave it a D-plus, praising none of the actors.

There were high hopes for *Monster-in-Law,* also released in 2005, which starred Jane Fonda as the mother of the man Lopez's character planned to marry. The movie marked Fonda's return to the big screen after a fifteen-year absence and was much anticipated. Lopez played a working-class girl, employed as a dog walker, who

Jane Fonda and Jennifer Lopez come face-to-face in a scene from Monster-in-Law.

is engaged to a doctor. Fonda's character is not fond of the match, and their antagonism toward each other is at the heart of the movie.

The resulting film about their family feud was uninspired, critics said. "There's nothing complicated about *Monster-in-Law,* a movie that will have you chuckling even as you recognize its total lack of originality, subtlety or honest feeling,"[62] said Rozen. The critic said Fonda easily out-acted Lopez in the film, as she gave her all to the nasty nature of her character while Lopez preferred only to pout and snarl in a dainty manner.

Not in It for Money

Even these pictures had a bright spot for Lopez, however. She was earning up to $12 million per film, a considerable sum for an actress who was popular with the public but suffered at the hands of critics. It was not only movies that were making Lopez rich, however. In 2004 she was the nineteenth richest person in America under forty, according to *Fortune* magazine, due in part to $300 million in revenue brought in by her fragrances and clothing lines. She seemed to be constantly in motion. "I've said my life is like a roller-coaster ride, but it's really more like a hamster

Even Lopez Stumbles

It seemed Lopez was an unstoppable force in the entertainment world, but even she could not prevent a virus from affecting her health. When she performed with her husband, Marc Anthony, at the Grammy Awards, a sore throat and swollen glands caused her to give a sub-par performance. Her doctor made her cancel a trip to London to promote the movie *Shall We Dance?* and she had to forego her European concerts as well, where she had planned to perform songs from her CD *Rebirth.*

She did make it to Germany to perform the song "Get Right" on the television show *Wetten, dass . . . ?* but still was not at 100 percent. She lost her balance, barely missed falling, and almost stepped on one of her backup dancers.

In An Unfinished Life, *Lopez worked with Academy Award winners Robert Redford (pictured) and Morgan Freeman.*

wheel," she said. "Going and going, doing and doing. What else is new?"[63]

Lopez insisted that she did not let money drive her career, however. There were reports that she cut her salary to $4 million in order to work with Robert Redford and Morgan Freeman on *An Unfinished Life*. The projects she did were not based on the amount of money she could make from them but on whether they interested her and were something she could wholeheartedly support. She noted that she turned down an idea to make a doll based on her image, even though it would likely be a moneymaker for her. She preferred to do things that stirred an interest inside her. "For me, it's not about a level of fame or celebrity," she said. "You're born, and you want to do it. That's what people don't understand. It's something that kind of lives inside you. My passion is not my salary."[64]

For the Record

One thing Lopez was passionate about was her singing. She knew there were people in the studio who could enhance her voice to make it sound better and that she could strike a chord with fans. It was always her goal to entertain the public, which she did, whether critics liked the way she did it or not. She may have not have had the vocal range of other singers, but that did not prevent her from doing her best and putting out songs that she thought others would enjoy.

Lopez offered remixes of her popular singles on *J to tha L-O! The Remixes* in 2002, and she proved her strength as a saleswoman as it reached number one on the Billboard 200. The new versions of songs on the CD were quite different from the originals, and revisions of songs like "I'm Real," "Ain't It Funny," and "Love Don't Cost a Thing" got new life from their refashioning. Some critics found it refreshing. "As a rule, 'remix' sets tend to be lame, money-mooching filler sets, but *J to tha L-O!* is the exception," wrote Michael Paoletta in *Billboard*.[65]

Others were not as enthusiastic about the CD or Lopez's singing ability. David Browne of *Entertainment Weekly* gave it a grade of D-plus. He harshly criticized her voice, saying, "The fad of rappers guesting on pop singles truly helps when it comes to Lopez, since you hear less of her."[66]

This Is Me

The Latin dance-pop sound of Lopez's first CDs was replaced by a different sound on *This Is Me . . . Then*, also released in 2002. The CD reflected Lopez's contentment at the time, as she was dating Affleck when she recorded the songs on the album. "Musically, Lopez channels her bliss into unabashedly nostalgic pop-soul confections with tangy shells and warm, sweet fillings,"[67] wrote Elysa Gardner in *USA Today*. The material flattered Lopez's delicate vocals, Gardner said, as it emphasized that she could be a strong woman as well as a feminine one. Its romantic overtones reflected Lopez's ability to continue to believe in love despite two failed marriages and a barrage of media attention that dogged her during her relationship with Affleck. The CD also reflected Lopez's reaction to her fame. In the song "Jenny from the Block" she emphasized that inside she was really the same girl that she had always been and that her success had not changed the person she was inside.

Everyone Knows Her Name

"Jennifer Lopez has reached that rare strata of super-celebrity where she's famous just for being famous."

—Jim De Rogatis, "J. Lo Has Little to Say and Not Much Voice to Say It With." http://www.jimdero.com/News2005/JLoReviewMar1.htm.

She again brought in guest artists to sing with her on this CD, a decision that Chuck Arnold of *People* magazine said was the right one. Her hip-hopping songs with LL Cool J, Jadakiss, and Styles were fun and upbeat, he said. However, Arnold was not as enthusiastic about Lopez's solo numbers. When she was on her own the quality quickly deteriorated, and her vocals sounded thin. He noted that the worst song on the CD was one in which she sang about her love for Affleck.

Rebirth

Although she had been criticized for the songs that reflected her private life, Lopez again got personal with her music when she released *Rebirth* two years later. She began recording after finishing a six-month vacation, the first extended break from work she had had in years. The break came as her relationship with Affleck was ending, and after both the vacation and the relationship were over she felt refreshed and revived. She was ready to start again. "I was ready to go back into the studio and start over," she said. "I just felt like it was a new day."[68]

Lopez knew exactly the type of sound she wanted the album to convey. She recorded fewer songs than she usually did when

Rapper Fat Joe performs with Jennifer Lopez on the Today *show.*

she made a CD, because she knew where she was going from the start. If she did not feel strongly about a song, if it did not move her, she rejected it even if it had the potential to be a hit. "In the past, I would usually record 18 to 22 songs and then narrow it down," she said. "This time I had grown more clear about what I wanted to do. I had been listening to older music—to the blues, to James Brown. It's not like I just turned left and did something different, but I adapted the sound."[69]

Rebirth included dance songs as well as a strong dose of love ballads. The album has a passionate sound, Lopez said, as she applied her life experiences to her music. She cowrote some of the material for the album, which had hints of nostalgia. She wanted to freshen her sound by leaning toward funk, with more horns and drums

The CD also had echoes of her first release, *On the 6*. It had the same executive producer and Anthony once again contributed musically by cowriting several songs. As on her previous albums, Lopez once again got an assist from some guest artists and producers. She did duets with rappers Fat Joe and Fabolous, and others contributing to the CD included Rodney Jerkins, Timbaland, and Big Boi.

The CD debuted at number two on the Billboard 200 chart when it was released in March 2005, but Lopez was outshown on her duet tracks by the superior voices of her partners, noted music critic Jim DeRogatis. He liked some of the CD's upbeat tracks, such as "Step into My World" and "Get Right," but criticized the CD for containing too many dull ballads and offering material that revealed little about Lopez as a person. "Lopez has very little to say on her fourth set of new material, and she says it in a slight and forgettable voice," he said. "And for all her talk of rebirth, she offers little insight into the inner workings of her soul."[70] David Browne of *Entertainment Weekly* criticized Lopez for trying to be all things to all people, from a hip-hop artist to a singer of ballads. The overly commercial result was watered-down emotion. "One gets the sense from *Rebirth* that Lopez wants her music to be inoffensive and as easy to swallow as baby food, all the better to reach as wide a consumer base as possible," Browne said. "Too bad, since somewhere inside Jennifer Lopez Inc. is a dancing queen still waiting to break out."[71]

A Friend in Fat Joe

For Jennifer Lopez's CD *Rebirth*, she did a song and video with Fat Joe called "Hold You Down." The lyrics spoke about their friendship, which is strengthened by their Latino roots. They had worked together on Lopez's first album. "That was back when everybody thought, Oh, she's just an actress who wants to make a record. But Fat Joe got down with me purely because I was Puerto Rican and from the Bronx. Just to rep for Latinos," Lopez said.

Over the years the two had become like *familia*, she said. "If he calls me and needs help, I'll do it if I can, and same way with him," she said. "So the song is like a love song, but it's our friendship song. It's about what we really mean to each other."

Quoted in Jenny Eliscu, "La Vida Lopez," *Cosmo Girl*, April 2005, p. 128.

Phase Two

Rebirth marked the beginning of a new phase in Lopez's personal life as well. While she was recording the CD she was dating Anthony, and they married in June 2004. Some questioned whether her marriage was too hasty, since it had been less than a year since her broken engagement to Ben Affleck. Lopez, however, was certain that her love life was finally heading in the right direction.

Anthony brought stability to Lopez's world. They shared a Latin background, a love for music, and a commitment to family. Anthony taught Lopez that less could be more. In his view fewer public appearances, a slower-paced career, and more quiet nights at home could be just as fulfilling as the whirlwind life she had been living.

Lopez called this period phase two of her life. She maintained her glamorous image but turned down the intensity level of her career. She still worked on movies, recorded songs, and began more business ventures, but her personal life was not open to public viewing as it had been in the past. Lopez's marriage to Anthony was a turning point in her life, as she eased into a much more subdued lifestyle that provided less fodder for media attention.

After the break she took before recording *Rebirth*, she realized she needed to strike more of a balance between work and her personal life. Work had been a constant for her and kept her life full, but she realized that a successful career would not ultimately be what she wanted to look back on when she thought about her life. "As you mature, you realize [work] is not going to make you happy and fulfilled," she said. "In 50 years, what's going to be there, your career or the people you formed relationships with?"[72] Her time away from work caused her to realize that she was still just the same girl she had always been, someone who wanted to make movies, sing, and dance. However, she now wanted to do it at a pace that allowed her to enjoy it.

Chapter 6

A New Outlook

Lopez had become an extremely successful mainstream artist. She had conquered movies, music, and business and had a glamorous image that shone on the red carpet. Even after reviews of her acting soured and her hot career as an actress cooled, Lopez had no regrets about the decisions she made. She had talent and was not about to let her career fade. There was no intimidating this girl from the Bronx.

She had always watched out for her career, and now she was just as consciously careful about her personal life. In addition, she embraced the Hispanic side of her heritage more fully, exploring it in movies and music. Anthony, himself an established singer on the Latin charts, helped bring out this side of his wife's identity. He worked on Latin-themed music and movies with her and also helped her set priorities in her hectic life. With Anthony, Lopez found balance between her busy career and a quiet life at home. She was still a sought-after actress and successful business woman but now had stability on the home front.

Settling In

Lopez changed her routine to suit her more settled lifestyle. She tried to be home by nine each night, when she would watch television and spend time with her husband. "I don't take phone calls after a certain time now," she said. "Before, people could call me at 2 or 3 in the morning and I didn't care. But it's different now. The most important thing is I need eight hours of sleep or else I'll lose my mind."[73]

When she was dating high-profile stars such as P. Diddy and Affleck, Lopez did not bother to adjust her schedule to avoid photographers. She took the lack of privacy in stride. Now, however, she made a conscious attempt to give her life a lower profile. She did not complain about the over-the-top attention she had received in the past but noted that she was now trying to avoid it. She was careful about where she went, how she traveled, and when she left.

When she was younger she had not realized how her actions had fed the public interest that contributed to her lack of privacy. Eventually her personal life began to overshadow the work she was striving so hard to be respected for, and she realized she needed to take responsibility for changing that. She had learned what could happen if she allowed herself to be too open and no longer wanted that to be part of her life. "The going-out-and-being-glam thing gets old fast," she said. "I'd rather have friends over, be with my niece, or be in the studio writing. People keep saying to me, 'You're not out there anymore.' And I say, 'That's because I don't want to be.'"[74] She realized she did not have to be constantly on the move. She compared herself to a hamster running on a wheel. "I learned I don't have to be on the wheel all the time," she said. "I just jump on when I feel like it."[75]

Quiet Romance

From the start Lopez and Anthony kept their romance and marriage very low-key. Before their wedding, when a reporter from the magazine *InStyle* noticed that Lopez was wearing a glittering diamond ring, Lopez would not admit that it was an engagement ring. She simply called it a gift.

While the pair had only a six-month courtship before their wedding, Anthony and Lopez had known each other for years. They had worked together on Lopez's first CD and dated briefly. After her breakup with Affleck they began seeing each other while both were living in Miami. Anthony asked Lopez to do a duet with him for his new album, *Amar sin Mentiras (To Love Without Lies)*, and they recorded "Escapemonos" ("Let's Escape"). While he called her his inspiration on the CD's credits, they said very little in public about their feelings for each other. Anthony was with Lopez while she prepared for a magazine photo shoot and made an appearance on the television show *Will and Grace*, even taking photos of her to record the occasion, but they did not come right out and say that they were a couple. "We have a great working relationship," Lopez said in an interview a few weeks before their wedding. "I have to keep my work and my personal life separate. Otherwise it gets blurry and it gets messy."[76]

In stark contrast to the elaborate and public ceremony that had been planned with Affleck, her wedding to Anthony was quiet, secretive, and a surprise. Lopez planned the wedding in three weeks, and few guests were told that the event would be a wedding. Rather, the couple asked guests to come to an afternoon party.

Sky's the Limit for This Star

"As the Bronx-born daughter of Puerto Rican immigrants, Lopez, 36, has an outsider's hunger and a native's assumption of infinite possibility. She works hard and dreams big."

—Josh Tyrangiel, "The Diva from the Block," *Time*, August 22, 2005, p. 45.

The couple invited forty close friends and family to the ceremony at her mansion in Beverly Hills. Lopez's mother, sister, and father attended, and after the guests had arrived Anthony told them that a wedding was going to occur. They were married in a brief ceremony, and guests were treated to a reception that included a dinner with lobster, caviar, and champagne. The event was small and intimate but sophisticated, and Lopez looked glamorous.

A few days after their wedding Anthony appeared on NBC's *Today* show and *The View* on ABC and refused to confirm that they were married. While Anthony did not speak publicly about his love for his wife, he stated it without words. At a concert in

Marc Anthony and Jennifer Lopez, singing together in 2007, tried to keep their romance and marriage quiet.

Miami Beach he wore a pendant engraved with "Jenny" and pointed to her as he sang "Nadie como Ella" ("Nobody like Her"). His public displays of affection were far from overstated, but he was showing that he cared for his wife by protecting her privacy.

He was also there to support her when she was at work. When Lopez visited Europe in late 2004 to promoted *Rebirth*, Anthony sat near and smiled at her while she sang a sample of songs from the album. When she taped an appearance on the French version of *American Idol* called *Star Academy* he was with her, and they left holding hands.

She was there for her husband when he was touring as well. When Anthony was performing the next summer, Lopez accompanied him and attended his shows. They kept her presence quiet until an appearance in Irvine, California, when Anthony brought her onstage for a quick wave and kiss.

When they went out, Lopez and Anthony made a conscious effort not to attract attention. A peaceful night out meant a quiet dinner for the pair. When they wanted to see the movie *Shrek 2* with some friends, they bought out almost every seat in the theater so they would not be besieged by fans. They then sneaked in through a back entrance.

Change of Pace

Although being subdued had never been Lopez's style, she now had a new attitude toward publicity. To keep things from getting out of hand, she shut the public out of her private life as much as she could. "Things get blown up by the press, and there's some things in life she wants to keep private," explained Leslie Sloan Zelnick, Lopez's spokesperson. "This is the way she wants to live her life."[77]

Lopez's determination to keep her private life to herself was a change for the actress, and some wondered if she was harming her career by taking herself out of the spotlight. Her intriguing personal life was part of her attraction as a celebrity, and by making herself less accessible she risked diminishing her value as a sought-after star.

"Her media strategy seems to be that less is more," noted Janis Min, editor of *Us* magazine. The media attention Lopez had received in the past had been excessive, Min admitted, recalling the embarrassment that Lopez's public relationship with Affleck had become, making her the punch line of jokes. She reflected that a quiet approach might not work for her, however, because of her love for publicity and her interesting life. "People love her because she's been out there and has a colorful life,"[78] Min said.

Big Business

Lopez had slowed things down with her career but had not stopped completely. She continued to record and look into movie projects because this is what she liked to do. It was difficult for her to choose which part of her career she enjoyed most. "All of the things I do come from this need I have to be creative, and I just try to do the things that make me happy and help me grow," she said. "It's not something you're choosing to do: It's something you have to do, want to do, and really need to get better at all the time. And that's how I feel about singing and acting and creating fashion and everything I do. It just lives inside me."[79]

Lopez continued to expand her business ventures, adding a fragrance called Still to her perfume line and introducing lingerie and a line of clothing with an urban chic look called Sweetface. At a fashion show in Manhattan she noted that the clothing line's name came from a nickname a former agent had used for her. The look reflected her style—glamorous, but with a street edge. By combining her upbringing in the Bronx with her style as a star, Lopez created a fashion line with a look that sold well. Other singers also had clothing lines, but they were not as popular as hers. In only four years Lopez had managed to build up the most successful clothing brand a music artist had introduced.

Embracing Her Heritage

Lopez found success with her clothing line by giving it a dose of her personality, and now she gave her career a new edge by emphasizing her heritage. In her movies, music, and business, she saw an opportunity to blend her Hispanic background with the work she loved to do. She turned to meaningful work that took her back to her roots.

Lopez's success in business helped her do this. With a fragrance line doing global sales in excess of $500 million, she had enough money to make the films she wanted. She could produce movies as well as act in them and had the freedom to be choosy about which movies she became part of.

It had been a phone call from one of her idols, Barbra Streisand, that emphasized to her the direction she should take with her career. She had sent Streisand a pair of scripts to look over, because Lopez hoped to work with her. Streisand read the scripts and replied that Lopez was too good for that material. Streisand's assessment of the material made Lopez rethink her career and concentrate on projects that were meaningful to her. She put up some of the financing for her next album and two movies, all of which reflected her Hispanic roots.

Second to None

"J. Lo's place on a list of most influential Hispanics is a no-brainer. Why? Because over a decade ago, she was an anonymous background dancer on [a] second-rated sketch-comedy show. Today she's known by two syllables. That's one less than Madonna, and, yes, Lopez is probably counting."

—Josh Tyrangiel, "The Diva from the Block," *Time*, August 22, 2005, p. 45.

For years Lopez had been working intensely and had her private life exposed. Now she wanted to return to what initially drew her to performing. She wanted to express herself creatively and take on projects that she believed in.

Making Movies

The first of these projects was a film with her husband, titled *El Cantante*. Lopez had been interested in making the movie for years and had recruited Anthony for the lead role back in 2002. Little did they know then, Lopez said, that they would be a couple when the film was finally made.

El Cantante tells the story of Hector Lavoe, who brought the salsa movement to the United States. Anthony had the title role and, in addition to producing the film, Lopez also played Hector's wife. The story has both proud and tragic moments as Hector's success as a musician becomes overshadowed by his drug abuse.

The film gave Anthony and Lopez the opportunity to work together, and both enjoyed it. Friends warned them that working together could strain their relationship and cause the line to blur between work and home, but they had no problems, Anthony said. To the contrary, it was a great experience for the couple.

While they enjoyed making the movie and Lopez was proud to make a film that featured the life of an influential Hispanic musician, the initial reviews for the movie were not complimentary.

It was criticized for the way the story was told and for the uncomfortable way Lopez and Anthony played their roles. "Lopez conjures up plenty of ferocity and street attitude as Puchi, but there's no shape, or power, to her wrath," wrote Robert Koehler in *Variety*. "Similarly, Anthony seems ill at ease."[80]

Latina Legend

"People love to see somebody who went from a modest family to fame and fortune. No matter what she's done that might not have been successful, the overall image of her is of the breakthrough Latina superstar."

—Howard Rubenstein, quoted in Cesar G. Soriano, "The Media Have Insatiable Appetite for J. Lo," *USA Today*, June 17, 2004, p. 1d.

While Lopez had hopes that the film would be well received, she was past worrying about what critics said. She was more focused on making movies that fit her interests. Another example of this was the movie *Bordertown*, which her company Nuyorican Productions helped produce.

The movie addresses the serious issue of kidnapping along the U.S. border with Mexico. Lopez played a journalist investigating a series of murders of women near the Mexican border in Texas. She had been interested in the role for years, ever since Gregory Nava had approached her about making the movie in 1998. He had directed her in her first big hit, *Selena*, and wanted her to be part of this enlightening film as well.

After hearing of the tragic crimes the movie focused upon, Lopez agreed that it was a film that should be made. She wanted to bring attention to the issue and pressure the Mexican government to bring those responsible to justice. Lopez's support for the film was rewarded. She received an Artists for Amnesty Award from Amnesty International for her work in bringing the issue to light.

Como Ama una Mujer

For several years Lopez and Anthony also worked together on her Spanish-language CD. She had recorded a few songs in Spanish before, but the CD *Como Ama una Mujer* (*How a Woman*

Amnesty International presents Lopez with the Artists for Amnesty Award for her work on the film Bordertown.

Home Again

Lopez returned to her old neighborhood to sign autographs when she was promoting *Como Ama una Mujer* (*How a Woman Loves*). Marc Anthony was with her when she appeared at a record store, and about five hundred people gathered to see her. Singing in Spanish had long been a goal of hers, said Lopez, who learned the language as an adult. She was thrilled to be back home, where her dreams began.

Loves) was entirely Latin-inspired. From the Spanish lyrics to the Latin tempos, it reflected a different side of Lopez.

She got the idea to make an album entirely in Spanish after recording a song with her husband for his album. Anthony was one of the producers for *Como Ama una Mujer*, and the music gave Lopez a chance to show her emotions, vulnerability, and passion. The motive behind making the album was not simply to make something commercially successful, she said, but something that she enjoyed creating. She wanted to do this project from the heart.

The album had romantic themes and dramatic ballads, and the result was not bad. The single "Qué Hiciste" ("What Did You Do?") became the first all-Spanish-language video to hit number one on the show *TRL* on MTV. The album hit number one on the Top Latin Albums chart and number twenty on the Billboard 200.

While Arnold noted in *People* magazine that ballads would never be her strength, he said she did well with the Latin rhythms. Anthony's assistance helped her easily make the transition from Jenny from the Block to Jenny from the Barrio, Arnold said. While the CD showed that she had some singing ability, *Entertainment Weekly* reviewer Chris Willman also noted that it lacked the muscle needed to carry off the passionate ballads. No matter what the reviewers said, however, Lopez had succeeded in making an album that made her proud.

Family Time

Lopez continued to move along with a number of projects geared toward both a mainstream audience and a Hispanic one. She gave advice to contestants on *American Idol* and introduced a reality series on MTV called *Dancelife*. She planned another album, one with a

Lopez visits MTV's TRL show. Her single "Qué Hiciste" became the first all-Spanish-language video to hit number one on the show.

dance-oriented sound and English lyrics. Another new perfume with a Latin-inspired name was also on the horizon, and there was also talk of Lopez's Nuyorican Productions company making television shows for Fox, including one about Latin nannies in Los Angeles.

Lopez's star status meant that she and Anthony moved in elite Hollywood circles, hanging out with couples such as Tom Cruise and Katie Holmes, Jim Carrey and Jenny McCarthy, and Victoria and David Beckham. However, while Lopez had many productions and movies on her schedule, she also wanted some things in life that were very traditional. Anthony had three children from previous relationships, and Lopez enjoyed being a step-mother to them. She and Anthony also hoped to have a child one day.

While her career was far from stalling, Lopez was through rushing from project to project. She treasured the time she had to spend with Anthony and her family. Lopez had a feeling of con-

In April 2007, singer Jennifer Lopez gave advice to contestants on American Idol.

Subdued Style

As Lopez changed her lifestyle from high-intensity to more subdued, she changed her style as well. The look was not as sexy as it once was but more serious and classic. The songs on her Spanish-language album *Como*

Ama una Mujer had a timeless, classic quality that influenced Lopez's look. Lopez said she was even interested in elegant touches such as hats and gloves, as well as clothing closed at the neck with a bow.

tentment when she considered her relationship with Anthony. They enjoyed both working together and being together as a couple. Once hesitant to discuss their relationship at all, she opened up a bit when discussing their happiness. "Marc and I are good partners," she said. "We love each other. We want to be the best person we can be for each other. And we work on that. That's what a real relationship is about to me."[81]

Lopez realized that she could not control the future, just hope for the best. She knew that she had not always made wise decisions but did not regret how she had lived her life. She never stopped trying, always did her best, and was satisfied with the way things were turning out for her. "You have your hopes and you have your dreams and you go for them. You never know what's gonna happen or what kind of path you're going to wind up going down. . . . I feel very fortunate and very thankful for the way things have gone."[82]

Notes

Chapter 1: "Jenny from the Block"

1. Quoted in Kate Meyers, "Not Just a Token Actress," *Entertainment Weekly*, December 1, 1995, p. 44.
2. Quoted in Katie Coyne, "'I Am a Good Girl!'" *Good Housekeeping*, June 2002, p. 86.
3. Quoted in Jenny Eliscu, "La Vida Lopez," *Cosmo Girl*, April 2005, p. 128.
4. Quoted in Elizabeth Kuster, "The Secrets of Jennifer Lopez," *Cosmo Girl*, June/July 2002, p. 86.
5. Quoted in Kuster, "The Secrets of Jennifer Lopez," p. 86.
6. Quoted in Anthony Bozza, "Jennifer the Conqueror," *Rolling Stone*, February 15, 2001, p. 44.
7. Quoted in Michelle Tauber, "Livin' la Vida Lopez," *People*, May 27, 2002, p. 112.

Chapter 2: Leading Lady

8. Roger Ebert, "*My Family*," *Chicago Sun-Times*, May 3, 1995. http://rogerebert.suntimes.com/apps/pbcs.dll/article?AID=%2F1 9950503%2FREVIEWS%2F505030301%2F1023&AID1=%2F 19950503%2FREVIEWS%2F505030301%2F1023&AID2=.
9. Ken Tucker, "'Money Train' Never Really Makes It Out of the Station," *Entertainment Weekly*, December 1, 1995. www.ew.com/ew/article/0,,299778,00.html.
10. Quoted in *People*, "Feeling the Heat," December 11, 1994, p. 157.
11. Roger Ebert, "*Jack*," *Chicago Sun-Times*, August 9, 1996. http://rogerebert.suntimes.com/apps/pbcs.dll/article?AID=/199 60809/REVIEWS/608090304.
12. Quoted in Dave Karger, "Biopicked for Stardom," *Entertainment Weekly*, August 9, 1996, p. 40.
13. Quoted in Jeffrey Ressner, "Born to Play the Tejano Queen," *Time Canada*, March 24, 1997, p.53.
14. Peter Travers, "*Selena*," *Rolling Stone*, April 17, 1997, p. 86.

15. Quoted in Degen Pener, "From Here to Divinity," *Entertainment Weekly*, October 9, 1998, p. 28.
16. Peter Travers, "Sex and the Action Hero," *Rolling Stone*, July 9, 1998, p. 145.
17. David Ansen, "The Fugitive Falls in Love," *Newsweek*, August 3, 1998, p. 54.
18. Lisa Schwarzbaum, "This Mortal Coil," *Entertainment Weekly*, April 18, 1997, p. 48.
19. Ressner, "Born to Play the Tejano Queen," p. 53.
20. Quoted in *People*, "Jennifer Lopez," May 12, 1997, p. 124.
21. Quoted in *People*, "Jennifer Lopez," May 10, 1999, p. 187.
22. Quoted in *Sunday Mirror* (London), "Jennifer Lopez: The Ego Has Landed," November 15, 1998. www.findarticles.com/p/articles/mi_qn4161/is_19981115/ai_n14483313/pg_1.
23. Quoted in *Sunday Mirror*, "Jennifer Lopez: The Ego Has Landed."
24. *Sunday Mirror*, "Jennifer Lopez: The Ego Has Landed."
25. Rick Bonino, "Glow? It's Just Her Ego Reflecting Off Her Head," *Spokesman Review*, January 23, 1998. www.findarticles.com/p/articles/mi_qn4186/is_19980123/ai_n11557999.
26. Quoted in Pener, "From Here to Divinity," p. 28.

Chapter 3: J. Lo

27. Quoted in Coyne, "'I Am a Good Girl!'" p. 86.
28. Quoted in Carla Hay, "Lopez Fulfills Music Dreams," *Billboard*, December 4, 1999, p. 22.
29. Quoted in *Jet*, "'Puffy' Combs and Jennifer Lopez," September 4, 2000, p.60.
30. Quoted in Kuster, "The Secrets of Jennifer Lopez," p. 86.
31. David Browne, "'6' and the Single Girl," *Entertainment Weekly*, June 4, 1999, p. 83.
32. Quoted in Larry Flick, "3rd Single Shows Lopez Has Legs," *Billboard*, January 8, 2000, p. 1.
33. Quoted in Bozza, "Jennifer the Conqueror," p. 44.
34. Chuck Arnold, "*J.Lo*," *People*, February 5, 2001, p. 35.
35. Erik Pedersen, "'Lopez' Adds Another Medium to Arsenal," *Hollywood Reporter*, international edition, November 20, 2001, p. 17.
36. Kuster, "The Secrets of Jennifer Lopez," p. 86.

37. Peter Travers, "Movies," *Rolling Stone*, September 14, 2000, p. 183.
38. Leah Rozen, *"Angel Eyes," People*, May 28, 2001, p. 36.
39. Roger Ebert, *"The Wedding Planner," Chicago Sun-Times*, January 26, 2001. http://rogerebert.suntimes.com/apps/pbcs.dll/article?AID=/20010126/REVIEWS/101260304/1023.
40. Quoted in Bozza, "Jennifer the Conqueror," p. 44.
41. Quoted in Juliann Garey, "J. Lo's Great New Year," *Redbook*, January 2002, p. 58.
42. Quoted in Coyne, "'I Am a Good Girl!'" p. 86.

Chapter 4: Public Mistakes

43. Quoted in Bozza, "Jennifer the Conqueror," p. 44.
44. Quoted in Bozza, "Jennifer the Conqueror," p. 44.
45. Quoted in Allison Samuels, "Beating a Bad Rap," *Newsweek*, June 3, 2002, p. 64.
46. Quoted in Garey, "J. Lo's Great New Year," p. 58.
47. Quoted in Samantha Miller et al., "Fast-Lane Love," *People*, August 12, 2002, p. 102.
48. Quoted in Chrissy Iley, "Lopez Lets Loose," *Harper's Bazaar*, December 2002, p. 190.
49. Quoted in Iley, "Lopez Lets Loose," p. 190.
50. Quoted in Garey, "J. Lo's Great New Year," p. 58.
51. Quoted in Jeannie Williams, "J. Lo and Fiennes (Ray-Fi) 'Maid' for Each Other," *USA Today*, December 10, 2002, p. 2d.
52. Quoted in Karen Thomas, "A Year of Bennifer Ends, a New One Looms," *USA Today*, December 19, 2003, p.5e.
53. Quoted in Greg Adkins et al., "Lopez on Lopez," *People*, April 26, 2004, p. 22.

Chapter 5: Cool Critics, Warm Public

54. Claudia Puig, "'Enough' to Make a Grown Critic Cry," *USA Today*, May 24, 2002, p. 14d.
55. Philip Kerr, "A Hit and Miss Affair," *New Statesman*, December 2, 2002, p. 39.
56. Leah Rozen, *"Maid in Manhattan," People*, December 23, 2002, p. 35.
57. Carl DiOrio, "Auds Give *Gigli* the Cold Shoulder," *Daily Variety*,

August 11, 2003, p. 9.

58. Leah Rozen, "*Gigli*," *People*, August 11, 2003, p. 33.

59. Peter Travers, "Jig's Up on *Gigli*," *Rolling Stone*, September 4, 2003, p. 151.

60. Leah Rozen, "*Shall We Dance?*" *People*, October 25, 2004, p. 33.

61. Roger Ebert, "*An Unfinished Life*," *Chicago Sun-Times*, September 9, 2005. http://rogerebert.suntimes.com/apps/pbcs.dll/article?AID=/20050908/REVIEWS/509080306/1023.

62. Leah Rozen, "*Monster-in-Law*," *People*, May 23, 2005, p. 31.

63. Quoted in Elysa Gardner, "Jenny on the Run," *USA Today*, February 23, 2005, p. 2d.

64. Quoted in Williams, "J. Lo and Fiennes (Ray-Fi) 'Maid' for Each Other," p. 2d.

65. Michael Paoletta, "*J to tha L-O!*," *Billboard*, February 16, 2002, p.19.

66. David Browne, "Pop/Rock/Rap," *Entertainment Weekly*, March 8, 2002, p. 74.

67. Elysa Gardner, "J. Lo's 'This is Me' Focuses Pop Soul on this Ben Dude," *USA Today*, November 26, 2002, p. 01d.

68. Quoted in Eliscu, "La Vida Lopez," p. 128.

69. Quoted in Gardner, "Jenny on the Run," p. 2d.

70. Jim DeRogatis, "J. Lo Has Little to Say and Not Much Voice to Say It With," *Chicago Sun-Times*, March 1, 2005. www.findarticles.com/p/articles/mi_qn4155/is_20050301/ai_n12829509.

71. David Browne, "Lo Impact," *Entertainment Weekly*, March 18, 2005, p. 64.

72. Quoted in Jennie Punter, "Rebirth of Cool," *Flare*, May 2005, p. 54.

Chapter 6: A New Outlook

73. Quoted in Karen S. Schneider et al., "Jennifer Lopez This Is Me . . . Now," *People*, March 7, 2005, p. 66.

74. Quoted in Merle Ginsberg, "What's Next for Jennifer Lopez?" *Harper's Bazaar*, December 2006, p. 272.

75. Quoted in Schneider, "Jennifer Lopez This Is Me . . . Now," p. 66.

76. Quoted in Degen Pener, "Moving to Her Own Beat," *InStyle*,

August 2004, p. 284.

77. Quoted in Donna Freydkin, "J. Lo Has a Lot to Promote—Just Not Herself." *USA Today*, September 14, 2004, p. 1d.

78. Quoted in Freydkin, "J. Lo Has a Lot to Promote," p. 1d.

79. Quoted in Eliscu, "La Vida Lopez," p. 128.

80. Robert Koehler, "*El Cantante*," *Variety*, September 25, 2006, p. 73.

81. Quoted in Margeaux Watson, "Born Again?" *Entertainment Weekly*, April 6, 2007, p. 40.

82. Quoted in Tom Jokic, "Jenny Gets Right," *Tribute*, April 2005, p. 22.

Important Dates

1970
Jennifer Lopez is born in the Bronx in New York.

1987
Lopez graduates from high school and attends college briefly. She leaves school to concentrate on dancing and acting.

1990
A job as a "Fly Girl" dancer on the show *In Living Color* takes Lopez from New York to California.

1995
Lopez is cast in her first film, *My Family*/Mi Familia. She also makes the action movie *Money Train*.

1996
Lopez is cast in the movie *Jack*, which stars Robin Williams.

1997
A role as slain Tejano singer Selena in the movie *Selena* earns Lopez praise and sets her on a course for stardom. She also appears in *Blood and Wine*, *Anaconda*, and *U Turn*. She marries Ojani Noa; they divorce after a year.

1998
A strong performance in *Out of Sight* seals Lopez's reputation as a bankable star. She also does voice work for the animated film *Antz*.

1999
Lopez's first CD, *On the 6*, is released.

2000
Lopez makes the thriller *The Cell*.

2001
She releases her second album, *J.Lo*, and the movies *Angel Eyes* and *The Wedding Planner*. She marries Cris Judd; they divorce after less than a year.

2002

J to tha L-O! The Remixes is released, as are her movies *Enough* and *Maid in Manhattan.*

2003

Gigli, with Ben Affleck, is released to awful reviews.

2004

Lopez marries Marc Anthony. Lopez makes a brief appearance in *Jersey Girl* and is also in *Shall We Dance?*

2005

Rebirth continues Lopez's music career, and she works with Jane Fonda in *Monster-in-Law* and Robert Redford in *An Unfinished Life.*

2006

Lopez works with her husband on the film *El Cantante.*

2007

Anthony assists Lopez on her CD *Como Ama una Mujer* (*How a Woman Loves*). The movie *Bordertown* is released.

For More Information

Books

Patricia J. Duncan, *Jennifer Lopez*. New York: St. Martin's, 1999. This paperback, available in English and Spanish, focuses on Lopez's early career and rise to stardom.

Heidi Hurst, *Jennifer Lopez*. San Diego, CA: Lucent, 2004. A biographical look at Lopez's life and career.

James Parish, *Jennifer Lopez—Actor and Singer*. New York: Ferguson, 2006. This book for teens follows Lopez's career.

Periodicals

Jenny Eliscu, "La Vida Lopez," *Cosmo Girl*, April 2005, p. 128.

Donna Freydkin, "J. Lo Has a Lot to Promote—Just Not Herself." *USA Today*, September 14, 2004.

Merle Ginsberg, "What's Next for Jennifer Lopez?" *Harper's Bazaar*, December 2006.

Web Sites

Entertainment Weekly (www.ew.com). Find news about Lopez and other celebrities.

Internet Movie Database (www.imdb.com). Search for Jennifer Lopez to find a list of her movie credits. The site also has her biography and a photo gallery.

Jennifer Lopez (www.jenniferlopez.com). On her official Web page at Epic records, hear Lopez's music and get information on her albums and movies. It also has ringtones, contests, and newsletters.

JLO by Jennifer Lopez (www.shopjlo.com). See the latest in Lopez's fashion collections and shop for clothing, perfume, and accessories.

People (www.people.com). Features the latest celebrity news. Search for Jennifer Lopez to find a biography and news about the star.

Index

Picture Credits

About the Author

Terri Dougherty is a reporter and writer who lives in Appleton, Wisconsin, with her husband, Denis, and their three children, Kyle, Rachel, and Emily. She enjoys going places with her family as well as playing soccer, jogging, and skiing. Her favorite Jennifer Lopez movie is *The Wedding Planner* and favorite Lopez song is "Qué Hiciste."